FAITH

STUFF

Increase Faith, Change Destiny!

STUDY GUIDE

By Phyllis Cook

COPYRIGHT PAGE

Table of Contents

INTRODUCTION WITH AUTHOR COMMENTS

God created all things including the laws that govern our universe. We can learn how to activate faith by better understanding the relationship between biblical principles and universal laws. The findings are incredible! Faith is not some spooky or mysterious nonsense. It is just common sense! It is easier to understand faith through chemical changes in atoms, the DNA of Christ, the effects of energy and light, time, eternity and the speed of light. All things are possible through Jesus Christ and there is scientific evidence to support it.

Your destiny is what you make it! You can create within yourself a mindset of success in every area of your life. Laws of physics come into play when faith is activated to change undesirable situations. You have the power to rewrite the rest of the script for your life!

ABOUT THE AUTHOR

The author, Phyllis Cook has earned a Pastoral Certification, an associate degree in Applied Science and has worked in a variety of volunteer ministries. She was a victim of depression that almost destroyed her life in her early adulthood. Through the gentle teaching of the Spirit of God, she was able to free herself from a cycle of self-defeat. She shares powerful and effective common sense that worked for her to restructure and renew her thinking. She explains how you can win the battle over the enemy of fear and depression; and tear down any barriers that can keep you from living a healthy lifestyle of victory, prosperity and real joy.

ACKNOWLEDGEMENT

I attribute and give all the credit and glory to God, the Father, Son and Holy Spirit. In Luke 4:18 (NKJV) Jesus said; "The Spirit of the Lord is upon me, because He has anointed me to preach the gospel to the poor; He has sent me to heal the brokenhearted, to proclaim liberty to the captives and recovery of sight to the blind, to set at liberty those who are oppressed."

CHOOSE TO CHANGE YOUR DESTINY

---◆---

Everything that is happening here on Earth, at this very moment is only temporary and subject to change. I believe that there are no coincidences, and whatever happens does so for a reason. Something or someone causes its state to be altered. Everything that we do begins in our thought life. The knowledge that we acquire and the thoughts that we are thinking in the present moment can create or affect our future in some way.

According to the Bible, knowledge comes with both good and evil. It is not just enough to fill our minds with information, but to know how to use the information wisely. The bible is the greatest book ever written. It gives us sound advice on how to make wise decisions for our own lives. It gives answers to all of life's questions and it is the doorway to our creator, God himself. He has supernaturally inspired civilization throughout time to record and preserve it. There are many historical stories that speak of his encounters with mankind. They show us his character, his likes, dislikes, and what He expects from us. They show what He wants to and can do for us. The Bible gives advice on how we can alter current situations to change our destiny as well as the destiny of others.

Philippians 4:8 (KJV) says, "Finally, brethren, whatsoever things are true, whatsoever things are honest, whatsoever things are just, whatsoever things are pure, whatsoever things are lovely, whatsoever things are of good report; if there be any virtue, and if there be any praise, <u>think on these things</u>."

In the preceding scripture, we are advised to fill our minds with thoughts that are good for us. We communicate with the world around us by what we see, hear, smell, taste and touch. Thoughts not only come to us through our five physical senses, but can develop as a result of a combination of sources.

Our emotional state greatly affects how we interpret and process thoughts. Depression, sadness, anger, fear and worry can have a tremendous influence on our thought life, and in turn direct are physical actions.

Depression can become relevant in a person's life due to a number of reasons. It may be a result of being hurt or rejected by others, the loss of a loved one, financial poverty or long term sickness. It can cause an attitude of bitterness to the point of creating one's own very lonely world, even to the point of shutting out God. Depression can cause people to become fearful of enjoying a life that God wants to give them.

We shape our own destiny by what we think, and what we do with what we think. Our minds were created to analyze situations and then offer solutions, whether they are good ones or bad ones. If we want to get good results, then we have to fill our minds with the right stuff.

For example, my son at three years old choked on a hard piece of candy that someone gave him. I had no clue what to do, so I began to panic. Somehow, in all the confusion of trying to help him, it came dislodged. It was a very helpless feeling and I did not want to ever go through that again. I began to have bad memories of the ugly episode and worried about it happening again. It bothered me every time my son was given a piece of candy. I finally decided to do something about my problem. I decided to take a CPR class, which included first aid for choke victims. I learned how to deal with the situation better, if it were to ever happen again. I supplied my mind with the right stuff to replace any fearful thoughts of panic.

The Bible warns us of a character who is doing his best to destroy us. He does this by negatively influencing our thought lives and we are at war with him whether we like it or not.

> 1 Peter 5:8 (NIV) warns us to be self-controlled and alert because our enemy the devil prowls around like a roaring lion looking for someone to devour.
>
> John 10:10 (KJV) is a scripture where Jesus tells us that the thief (Satan) comes to steal, kill and destroy.
>
> Ephesians 6:11-13 (KJV) says, "Put on the whole armor of God that ye may be able to **stand against** the wiles of the devil, for we wrestle not against flesh and blood, but against principalities, against powers, against the rulers of the darkness of this world, against spiritual wickedness in high places."

This last scripture tells us that we are in a battle with enemies that we can't see in the natural. We can see the results that they cause, but not the actual enemy. Scripture also tells us how to deal with them.

What we do with this biblical information is very important and can determine our destiny.

> We could reject the information, deny that there is an enemy and do nothing about it.
>
> We could accept it as true, and worry that the enemy will destroy us.
>
> We could believe it as true, and find out how to put on the armor of God to protect ourselves.

7

The more information that we have, the better equipped we are in dealing with spiritual forces. The Bible has a lot of the information that we need. We can learn to recognize the influences of Satan and how to defeat him in our own life.

Let's take the story of Adam & Eve in the Garden of Eden. God gave them permission to eat of every tree in the garden except from the tree of knowledge for good and evil. He said that if they did, they would die.

Satan (who is also referred to as Lucifer) convinced Eve to disobey God's order and steal the forbidden fruit that was not meant for them. Satan lied and told her that she would not die, and that she would become as gods knowing good and evil. Satan tricked her into thinking that she was an inferior being, and that God was holding out on her. He had to convince her that she had something wrong with herself, that she was missing something. She began to analyze and process all the information he gave her. Maybe she thought, "Are you saying I'm ignorant? I didn't know I was! I don't want to be ignorant! That's not fair, I want to be smart too! Did God cheat me out of something?" Maybe she looked at the tree differently now, thinking, "What are my consequences if I eat that fruit? Sounds like to me, according to Satan, God is holding out on me! Will I really die like God said? What is dying? Is it all that bad to die?". Satan caused her to begin to doubt God!

Eve did not understand what death was. How could she, since she had never experienced it! She had no idea that death would separate them both from God and his sources. For example, when a loved one dies, they become separated from us. We can't see them, hear them, touch them or enjoy their presence. They are no longer a part of our world of living atoms. We are separated from them.

If you were to separate a tree branch from a tree, it would begin to shrivel up and eventually die. It cannot survive by itself and is no longer a part of the tree. It needed to stay connected to the root, the heart of the tree to continue to live. It had no way of absorbing, accessing or enjoying the life-giving nourishment from the sun, soil and rain to keep it alive.

For both Adam and Eve, they would become more like the devil, who had already alienated himself from God. Satan has been trying to exalt himself to be like God, but he can't!

In Isaiah 14:14 (NIV) Satan said, "I will ascend above the tops of the clouds; I will make myself like the most high!" But in the next verse it says, "You are brought down to the realm of the dead, to the depths of the pit!"

There is only one God. We have no power or ability in ourselves apart from God to live forever and we cannot be God. God is our source of life.

The story of Adam and Eve marked the beginning of a hereditary system of unbelief that is still going on today. Satan did not make them disobey, all he could do was to influence their thoughts by giving bad advice. This is how he still works today.

Adam and Eve became afraid to be in the presence of God. They distanced themselves from their Lord and provider by what they did. Their perfect union with God had been broken. The outcome of the story is that the death sentence would be passed on to all mankind throughout time.

We all eventually physically die and become disconnected from everything around us. It means we cannot see, hear, touch or enjoy fellowship with our loved ones, or enjoy the things of this world that were created by God.

Satan's plan was, and still is to sever mankind's relationship with God, and in turn would lead to our total destruction. We are all in a spiritual battle with him and his band of rebels rather we like it or not. His future is very grim, and he wants to take as many of us as he can down with him. Now that we have the ability to choose good and evil, he tries to get us to choose a destructive lifestyle apart from our creator with his trickery and deceit.

Isaiah 14:12-16 (KJV) says, "How are thou fallen from heaven, O Lucifer, son of the morning! How art thou cut down to the ground, which didst weaken the nations! For thou hast said in thine heart, I will ascend into Heaven, I will exalt my throne above the stars of God. I will sit also upon the mount of the congregation, in the sides of the north. I will ascend above the heights of the clouds. I will be like the most High. Yet thou shalt be brought down to hell, to the sides of the pit. They that see thee shall narrowly look upon thee, and consider thee, saying, "Is this the man that made the earth to tremble, that did shake kingdoms?"

Revelation 20:10 (KJV) is written of things to come and says, "And the devil that deceived them was cast into the lake of fire and brimstone, where the beast and false prophet are, and shall be tormented day and night forever and ever."

Revelation 20:15 says, "And whosoever was not found written in the book of life was cast into the lake of fire."

These verses that are found in the book of Revelation are bad news for those who choose to ignore them, but they are good news for those whose names are written in the "Lambs Book of Life." They are comforted in knowing they will be spared from this ordeal and that the enemy will someday be totally defeated.

Revelation 12:10-11 (KJV) says, "And I heard a loud voice saying in Heaven, now is come salvation and strength and the kingdom of God, and the power of his Christ: for the accuser of our brethren is cast down, which accused them before our God day and night. And they overcame him (Satan) by the blood of the lamb and by the word of their testimony; and they loved not their lives unto the death."

Revelation 21:4 (KJV) says, "And God shall wipe away all tears from their eyes; and there shall be no more death, neither sorrow, nor crying, neither shall there be any more pain: for the former things are passed away."

What a time that will be. God has a wonderful plan waiting for all those who make the decision to follow Him.

Matthew 16:26, "For what is a man profited, if he shall gain the whole world, and lose his own soul? Or what shall a man give in exchange for his soul?"

The ultimate goal for every one of us should be in determining the destiny of our own souls. It is absolutely the most important and critical decision that we are to ever make in our entire lives, forever.

Questions Chapter 1

1. In order to be successful in our future, we must do something while in our _____ state.

2. Our minds were created to analyze situations and then offer solutions, whether they are _____ ones or _____ ones. If we want to get good results, then we have to fill our minds with the right stuff.

3. Philippians 4:8 (KJV) says, "Finally, brethren, whatsoever things are true, whatsoever things are honest, whatsoever things are just, whatsoever things are pure, whatsoever things are lovely, whatsoever things are of good report; if there be any virtue, and if there be any praise, _____ on these things."

4. Ephesians 6: 11-13 tells us, "Put on the whole armor of God that ye may be able to **stand against** the wiles of the devil, for we wrestle not against flesh and blood, but against principalities, against powers, against the rulers of the darkness of this world, against spiritual wickedness in high places."
We are in a battle with something we can't see. We can see the results that is caused, but not the actual enemies. If the above scripture is true, what should we do? Choose the best answer.
    _We could reject the information, deny that there is an enemy and do nothing about it.
    _We could accept it as true, and worry that the enemy will destroy us.
    _We could believe it as true, and find out how to put on the armor of God to protect ourselves.
    (The more information that we have, the better equipped we are in dealing with spiritual forces.)

5. Satan did not make Adam & Eve disobey God. All he could do was influence

their _____. This is how he still works today.

6. Revelation 20:10 and 15 is bad news for those who choose to reject the call of God. But it is good news for those whose names are written in the "Lambs Book of Life." They are comforted in knowing they will be spared from this ordeal and that the enemy will someday be totally _____.

7. According to the chapter, what should be the ultimate goal for every one of us in determining our destiny? The answer is also found in John 3:16-17 and Romans 10:13.

EMOTIONAL AFFECTS ON THE BODY

―――❧―――

Our thoughts exist as real material substance of some kind, since they can reside in our memory banks, and we can recall them over and over again.

They cause chemical reactions in the body, especially when they involve intense emotions. Negative emotions like depression and stress can cause a number of health problems. Fear can bring on heart palpitations and anxiety attacks; sad or hurtful experiences produce tears; anger can raise the blood pressure; embarrassment causes the face to flush; funny and unexpected surprises make us laugh; and joy brings on a smile. Our emotions and thoughts have an affect in the realm of physical substance, especially within our own physical bodies. We need faith! Faith works by giving hopes and dreams a chance! It has a positive affect on our thoughts and emotions because we are anticipating something good to happen in the near future. Without faith, the affects on our bodies can be devastating.

Here are some of the affects that I am aware of that are associated with being in a depressed or despairing state of mind.

No ambition

No confidence

Preoccupation and fear of death or the unknown

Thoughts of a gloomy future with no reason to want to live

Self-condemnation and a feeling of unworthiness

Feelings of having no power in one's own life

Pre-occupation that the worst is always going to happen

Fear of failure – or that making any changes could make things worse

Fear of losing control

Suicidal thoughts

Extreme sadness that won't go away

Low resistance to sickness

No energy / complete exhaustion

Many unrealistic phobias

Nightmares

Insomnia

Poor appetite or eating all the time

Ulcers

Anxiety attacks

Heart palpitations, lightheadedness

Low blood sugar

Feeling unsociable

Vitamin deficiencies

Light or sound sensitivity

Many of us go through some of these problems from time to time, but when they are continuous and overwhelming, they prevent us from living a healthy, wholesome lifestyle.

Proverbs 17:22 tells us that a merry heart is good like a medicine and that a broken spirit dries up the bones. Life giving blood cells come from the bone marrow. Experimental work has been done to show how different kinds of emotions can affect our blood cells. Emotions such as sadness, fear, anger and love affect blood cells by slightly changing their shape. Other experimental studies have proven that the emotional response of laughter can also have a significant effect on the body.

Physical exercise is one way to relieve stress. Laughter can be considered a physical exercise in faith. It can be an easy and fun way to relieve stress on our bodies. Positive emotions like laughter causes the body to release endorphins that relieve pain. There have been reports of people who claim that they have recovered from a serious illness using laughter as part of their therapy.

Our thoughts affect our emotional state, and in turn affect our health. Sometimes it takes healing of the mind and emotions before other physical symptoms will disappear.

Questions Chapter 2

1. The author thinks that thoughts are real material substances in our memory banks because we can _____ them over and over again

2. Our emotions and thoughts have an effect in the realm of physical substance. Name a couple of positive and negative emotions that can have an effect on the body and mind. What are some effects of each?

3. Can symptoms such as a low energy level, poor appetite, insomnia and ulcers be a sign of depression, yes, or no?

4. Can positive thoughts affect our health and can we improve our health by changing the way we think?

5. We can have feelings of love and affection towards another. We can also choose to show love towards another as an action. God tells us to show Godly love towards one another (as an action that we do). Can this type of action cause changes to the well-being of another? What about the person carrying out the love action? What is your opinion?

RECOGNIZING THE ENEMY

———⟨◆⟩———

Ordinarily, we as humans are in control of our thought life and decide how thoughts are to be stored in our memory banks. But for a person that is plagued by a negative thought pattern, it may be very difficult and frustrating. Unfriendly and tormenting thoughts can seem to pop into the imagination out of nowhere causing confusion and despair.

In Matthew, Chapter 16 (NIV), there is a story where Jesus explains to his disciples what is about to happen to Him. He was to be put to death, and be raised again on the third day. Peter was very distressed hearing that Jesus was to die and in verse 22, he spoke what was on his mind. He said, "Never Lord! This shall never happen to you!." Jesus turned to Peter and said, "Get behind me, Satan: You are a stumbling block to me….". In modern terms, Jesus spoke to Peter, but He rebuked an invisible presence He called Satan. He recognized that Satan gave thoughts to Peter. Peter gave into the thoughts and spoke them without realizing what he was doing. Peter did not understand that Jesus had to be put to death in order for salvation to come to mankind. If he would have known, he would not have yielded to Satan and spoke what he did. Jesus knew that Satan influences thoughts. Jesus and Satan both know that thoughts when spoken can make a difference between life and death.

Our minds process most things in question form. The key to overcoming hopelessness is to think questions through in such a way as to get positive answers. If you ask yourself a self-condemning question, you will get a self-condemning answer. Some obvious questions for someone caught up in a negative thought pattern may be questions like the following: "What is wrong with me? Am I going crazy? How could I be so stupid? Why can't I control my mind? Why does this always happen to me?" Pay attention to what questions you use to analyze your thoughts. If they are not producing the results that you need, then develop more productive questions to ask yourself. Ask God, where do these thoughts come from and how can they be stopped? Then search the scriptures for the answers. For example, in looking at the preceding scriptures where Jesus addressed the words spoken by Peter, our two questions were answered. First, Jesus blamed Satan as the source of what Peter thought and said. Secondly, Jesus showed us how He dealt with the situation.

There are evil spirits that can impress thoughts to our minds without us physically seeing or hearing them. They communicate and do their dirty work in the invisible spirit realm. The good news is that we can fight back and take control. Jesus did, and so can we! The Bible gives us advice on how to deal with these enemies.

2 Corinthians 10:3-5 (NIV) says, "For though we live in the world, we do not wage war as the world does. The weapons we fight with are not the weapons of the world. On the contrary, they have divine power to demolish strongholds. We demolish arguments and every pretension that sets itself up against the knowledge of God, and we take captive every thought to make it obedient to Christ."

James 4:7 (KJV) says, "Submit yourselves therefore to God. Resist the devil, and he will flee from you."

If the bible tells us that we can resist and run the devil off, then we can. There is an episode recorded in Matthew 4:5-11, where Jesus was confronted by Satan to be tempted. It was one of the greatest challenges ever recorded in

19

history. One temptation (of three) was where Satan tried to provoke Jesus into throwing himself down from a very high pinnacle of the temple and expect God's angels to save Him from death. But Jesus won the match when He resisted the challenge and responded with God's written word. "Thou shalt not temp the Lord thy God." If He had done what Satan told him to do, He would have voluntarily put himself under the authority and obedience of Satan.

Satan also took Jesus to a very high mountain and told Him that he would give Him rule over every kingdom if He, Jesus would worship him (Satan). Jesus resisted the challenge again and responded with God's written Word. He did not give into the terms of Satan or put himself under the authority of Satan. Instead, He told Satan to get lost and that He would continue to serve and obey God. Eve on the other hand, when tempted by Satan gave in and he defeated her. Jesus came to restore our position with the Father by defeating Satan for us.

There are people everywhere who are defeated by Satan because they don't understand what is happening to them or what to do about it. Satan bombards their imagination with harmful or even suicidal thoughts and they don't know why. First, these thoughts do not come from God because God does not give a spirit of fear. Secondly, God's gift to us is a spirit of power, love and a sound mind according to 2 Timothy 1:7. People who are victimized by negative and harmful thoughts all the time are being influenced by the enemy. If Satan can convince them that they are useless or inferior, he then can gain control of what they dwell on. If the mind doesn't know of any healthier alternatives to think on, it dwells on the only negative thoughts that it hears from Satan. It must be filled with other more positive and productive thoughts.

For example, 2 Timothy 1:7 says that God gives us a spirit of power, love and a sound mind. Take it by faith, not feeling, and trust God. Read it, analyze it and think about it often. At first, the mind and emotions may not understand the reality of this statement. But the Word is like seeds that you plant in a garden. The transformation takes root and starts deep down in your spirit and eventually works its way into the mind and emotions, just like a seed when planted in the ground can't be seen till it breaks through the ground. The truth is, that God wants all of us to live a full and happy life. Jesus himself said, "I have come that ye may have life and have it more abundantly."

Isaiah 7:14-15 tells us that God's Son (or own seed), Jesus would know to choose good over evil. It doesn't matter who we are, or what we have done in the past. It is because of who Jesus is and what He has done. He was tempted with thoughts too. He's been there! He used the Word of God, and said to Satan, "It is written." He recognized the enemy and knew how to deal with him. That's why He can help. He is our friend and counselor and through Him we can develop a victorious lifestyle.

Questions Chapter 3

1. According to Matthew 16:21-23, Jesus said, "Get thee behind me, Satan..." Can Satan transmit a thought to one's mind, yes, or no?

2. In Matthew 16:22, Peter said, "Be it far from thee, Lord, this shall not be unto thee." If Peter would have understood why Jesus had to die on the cross, would he have accepted the thought from Satan and spoke it, yes or no?

3. Thoughts when spoken could make a difference between _____ and _____.

4. If Jesus would have done what _____ told Him to do in the temptations of Matthew 4:4-11, He would have voluntarily put himself under the authority, obedience, power, or submission of _____.

5. Do you think that Eve recognized Satan as an enemy? 1 Timothy 2:14 has an answer.

6. Did Jesus recognize that Satan was an enemy?

7. How did Jesus win the match with Satan regarding the two temptations? He resisted the challenge from Satan and responded with Gods written _____.

8. We can come against enemy attacks the same way as Jesus did. James 4:7 tells us to _____ to God, _____ the devil, and he will _____ from us.

WORDS RELEASE POWER

In the world in which we live, we can take a thought or an idea and physically take the necessary steps to change our circumstance. For instance, if I need to get my bills paid, they would not get paid until I physically wrote out the checks and mailed them or paid them by other means. If I have a dream that I would like to come true, I would need to carry out the steps that would cause my dream to come true. This is something that I must physically do in the natural. We have to make a physical move in order for it to begin to become a reality.

We live in a world of wonderful wireless technology. We can send information through the air from a computer in one room, to a printer in another room of our home or office without the use of wires. We can communicate with others around the world through wireless cell phones. We can't see our words traveling through the air or see how the communication works, but we know it does.

Let's take the subject of sound. Sound is caused by vibration and it needs something to carry it. It cannot travel in a vacuum. It travels by air molecules bumping other air molecules. This chain reaction passes the sound. We can't see this happening, but we know it does because we hear the sound. The sound vibrates our inner eardrum, which sends a signal to our brain. Our brain interprets the information, converts it, and stores it in our memory banks. Every time we need to recall the information, our brain will present it to us in a form that we can understand.

When we speak, we are not taking the thought out of our memory banks. We are replicating or reproducing the original message. The reproduction is what is converted into sound waves and voiced by our vocal cords. But, the original message is still there.

When we speak our thoughts, we can make an impact in the world around us to change our circumstances. The bible tells us that words whether spoken by us or by God, himself, can be very powerful.

Words can make or break us according to the bible.

Proverbs 18:21 (KJV) says, "Death and life are in the power of the tongue."

Matthew 12:36 (KJV) is where Jesus said, "But I say unto you, that **every idle word that men shall speak**, they shall give account thereof in the day of judgment. For **by thy words** thou shalt be justified, and by thy words thou shalt be condemned."

He also said in Matthew 15:11 (KJV), "Not that which goeth into the mouth defileth a man; but that which **cometh out of the mouth**, this defileth a man."

Jesus is saying here that you can defile yourself by what you say. If you can be ruined by what you say, then you can be saved by what you say. He tells us words make a difference

Romans 10:8-10 (NKJV) says, "But what does it say? The word is near you, in your mouth and in your heart, that is, the word of faith which we preach: that if you **confess with your mouth** the Lord Jesus and believe in your heart that God has raised Him from the dead, you will be saved. For with the heart one believes unto righteousness, and **with the mouth confession is made unto salvation**." Verse 13 says, "For whoever **calls** on the name of the Lord shall be saved."

God's words are so powerful that they can set men and women free.

God said in Isaiah 55:11 (KJV), "So shall my word be that goes forth from my mouth; It shall not return to me void, But **it shall accomplish what I please, and it shall prosper in the thing for which I sent it.**"

In John 8:31-32 (NKJV) Jesus said, "If **you abide (or take) in my word**, you are my disciples indeed. **And you shall know the truth, and the truth shall make you free.**"

There are many scriptures in the bible that show us that the Word of God can change things. Jesus is our main spokesman / mouthpiece / Word from God. He was, and is God representing himself in human form as the person, Jesus. He existed in the beginning and spoke everything into existence.

John 1:1-4 and 14 (NIV) says, "In the beginning was the Word, and the Word was with God, and the Word was God. He was with God in the beginning. Through Him all things were made; without Him nothing was made that has been made. In Him was life, and that life was the light of men."

Verse 14, "The **Word became flesh and made his dwelling among us**. We have seen his glory, the glory of the one and only, who came from the Father, full of grace and truth."

Hebrew 11:1-3 (NKJV) says, "Now faith is the substance of things hoped for, the evidence of things not seen. For by it the elders obtained a good report. Through faith, we understand that **the worlds were framed by the Word of God**, so that the things which are seen were not made of things which do appear" (or are visible).

The life of Jesus is the **visible evidence** of the power and love of God manifest in human form.

He cursed a fig tree and it withered at the roots - Mark 11:21

He stilled a storm - Mark 4:39

He multiplied 5 loaves of bread & 2 fish to feed five thousand - Mark 6:41-43

He multiplied 7 loaves of bread & a few fish to feed four thousand - Mark 5-9

He walked on water - Matthew - 14:29

Healed a blind man - Mark - 10:52

Healed a crippled man by telling him to rise up and walk - John 5:8

He healed a father's son for him - John 5:50

He cast out a deaf and dumb spirit - Mark 9:25

He cast the devil out of a wild man - Mark 5:6-13

He cast a devil out of a woman's daughter without going to her - Mark 7:29

He raised the ruler of the synagogues' daughter from the dead - Mark 5:41

He raised a friend from the dead after he had been dead 3 days - John 11:43-44

A woman with a rare blood disease was healed instantly when she touched his garment - Mark 5:30-34

The Bible says, "As many as touched Him were made whole" in Mark 6:56

Throughout history, God has blessed those that trust and obey Him. Abraham and David are good examples of men who took God at his word and walked closely with Him. They were blessed with great wealth, prosperity and well-being.

As Gods people go out and speak about His Word around the world, it miraculously affects lives. It has the capacity to get the heart right, and if the heart gets right, it will desire the right things. Psalms 37: 3-5 tells us that we can have our hearts desire.

Psalms 37:3-5 (NKJV) says, "Trust in the Lord, and do good. Dwell in the land, and feed on his faithfulness. Delight yourself also in the Lord, **and He shall give you the desires of your heart.** Commit your way to the Lord, trust also in Him, and He shall bring it to pass."

Questions Chapter 4

1. In Matthew 12:36 (KJV), Jesus said, "But I say unto you, that every idle word that men shall speak, they shall give account thereof in the day of judgment. For by thy words thou shalt be justified, and by thy words thou shalt be condemned." He also said in Matthew 15:11 (KJV), "Not that which goeth into the mouth defileth a man; but that which cometh out of the mouth, this defileth a man." Jesus said that men shall be held accountable for every idle word they speak, and that words we speak can defile us. Does this mean that words have power?

2. If I have a dream that I would like to come true, I would need to carry out the steps that would cause my dream to come true. This is something that I must physically do in the natural. Can speaking words be considered a physical action?

3. Hebrew 11:11-3 says, "… we understand that the worlds were framed by the Word of God." John 1:14 says, "The Word became flesh and made his dwelling among us." Jesus is the Word of _____ and He is _____ representing his self in human form.

4. Do you think speaking contrary to the Word of God is resisting God instead of Satan?

5. As Gods people go out and speak His Word around the world, it miraculously affects lives. It has the capacity to get the heart right, and if the heart gets right, it will desire the right things. We can have the _____ of our heart, according to Psalms 37: 3-5.

6. In your own words, name something you read from the Bible or that God showed you in some other way that ministered or helped you with a problem in your own life.

EXISTENCE

There are many fascinating stories in the bible that some scientists believe are impossible to have happened. Yet, there are scientific studies in today's world proving more and more that these stories could have happened, and that all things are possible. In this section, I would like to take a look at some universal laws created by God himself to prove that the days of miracles are not over yet.

We can change undesirable circumstances by changing the way we think. Nothing is by chance, and life itself is affected by choices that we make every second of our lives. Even if we have failed in the past, we can improve our future.

God is the creator of all substance and everything exists because He spoke his thoughts into existence. He established the laws of the universe that keep the planets and stars in orbit. The earth is the right distance from the sun, and the moon is the right distance from earth. The earth has ideal temperatures for sustaining life. It also has the right atmospheric mixture of gases, and it has a magnetic field that protects us from to much sun. All of creation is working together in perfect harmony.

Everything is made up of a mixture of different chemicals. Depending on how those chemicals are mixed together and the amounts used determine what kind of substance it is. For example, we combine different chemical elements together all the time to make products like prescription drugs, cosmetics, and household products such as soaps and cleaners. We can and do physically change substances into other substances all the time.

Everything is made up of atoms. Atoms are made up of subatomic parts: protons, neutrons, electrons and some other smaller particles that science is trying to learn more about. *The ingredients in all atoms are identical*. There are many different kinds of atoms. What makes one atom different from another is the amount of each kind of ingredient in the atom. The number of protons, neutrons and electrons in the atom determines what substance it is.

Definition: Positively charge protons and neutrons with no-charge are compacted together in the center of the atom called the nucleus. Electrons are the negatively charged particles that orbit around the nucleus. Protons and electrons are opposite charges and attract to each other.

Atoms bind together with other atoms to make up what is called a molecule. A group of molecules are what makes up a chemical product that we see. Let's take water for an easy example. There are two types of atoms involved in producing water.

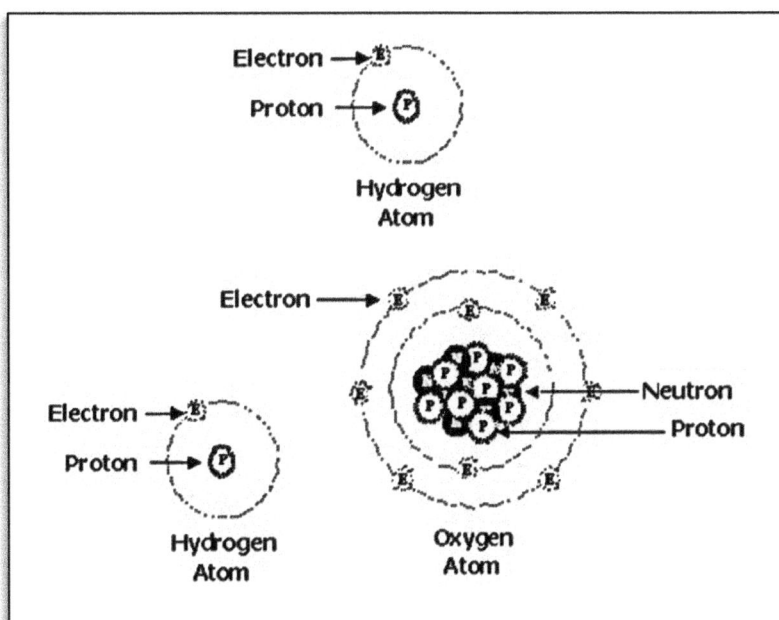

Electron →
Proton →
Hydrogen
Atom

Electron →
Proton →
Hydrogen
Atom

Electron →
Neutron
Proton
Oxygen
Atom

When the two types of atoms combine, they form what's called a molecule. Each molecule is made up of 2 Hydrogen atoms and 1 Oxygen atom. Each Hydrogen atom has 1 proton, 1 electron and no neutron whereas the Oxygen atom has 8 protons, 8 electrons and 8 neutrons. Both types of atoms have the same types of ingredients, but the Oxygen atom has more of each type of substance and therefore has a stronger energy force or attracting force than the Hydrogen atom. So it attracts or pulls toward itself the electrons from the Hydrogen atoms that are nearby. The result is that the 2 types of atoms bond together (like 2 magnets do) by the attracting force that is between them.

We can change substances into other kinds of substances just by combining different kinds of atoms. Science agrees that chemical reaction can change things into other things. We have the ability to change things into other things. So, if we can change things into other things, then we should know that God also has this ability -- scientific facts prove it.

All the miraculous stories of the Bible could have and did happen. God is the designer of the world and just by altering chemical properties He can change it to be whatever it needs to be.

Questions Chapter 5

1. Everything on Earth is made up of Atoms. The ingredients in atoms are identical. How do atoms bond together to make up the molecules that make up a chemical substance? Choose one answer.

    A. They don't

    B. By the attracting force (magnetic pull) between them

    C. Scientists don't know yet

2. Scientific research regarding chemical changes shows us that we do not have the ability to change things into other things and neither does God. Is this true or false?

3. Who established the laws of the universe in the first place, mankind or God?

4. Briefly study a supernatural or healing event from the Bible. You can find some from the list below, or look up an event from the present. Some of the incidences could have involved the help of angels. These stories help to increase faith!

Sun-dial turned 10 degrees backward, 2 Kings 20:10-12

Sun stood still, Joshua 10:13

Unhurt by the fiery furnace, Daniel 3:15-28

Daniel protected in the lion's den, 6:16-24

Burning bush not affect by fire, Exodus 3:2-4

Jesus raises the dead, John 11:43-44

Jesus walked on water, (Peter also walked on water), Matthew 14:25-31

Supernatural prison release, Acts 16:25-26

There are numerous stories throughout the Bible on healing. A lot of them are in Matthew, Mark, Luke and John.

UNIVERSAL LAW

Understanding a little bit about universal laws can strengthen ones faith to believe that all things are very much possible. In Matthew 21:21-22, Jesus tells us that if we have enough faith and do not doubt, we could go as far as to command a mountain to be cast into the sea and it would obey. He tells us in the scriptures that faith in God is the key to commanding the force of universal laws to go to work on our behalf.

Isaac Newton, the famous mathematician discovered three laws of motion that I think are excellent examples for explaining how we can change our world around us.

Here are the three laws.
1st law - Every object is in motion, and will remain in that state of motion until another external force is applied to it.
2nd law – Mass times Acceleration equals Force.
It is stated as an equation: M x A = F.
3rd law - For every action, there is an equal and opposite reaction.

Everything that exists is in motion. The sun, moon, stars, even our automobiles as they sit in our driveways are all in motion. Everything on Earth is moving along with the Earth around the Sun at the same rate as the Earth we stand on. If we see an object begin to move, it is in reality just accelerating. Its speed and/or direction of motion, and its relation to everything around it are what changes.

The first law says that **everything is moving or in motion, and will remain that way until an external force is applied.** In other words, it will remain in its present state of movement with the Earth until it is either pushed or pulled with a greater force. A force is the pull (attraction) or push (repulsion) between objects.

A good example of this law is in what happens in a tug of war contest. If both teams were to continually have an equal force, neither one of them would be able to win the game. Their state would stay the same. One of the teams must exert more force against the other team to pull (or move) the other team over the line.

The second law is a formula stating that **force equals the mass times acceleration**. We will get into more detail on this one later.

Let's go on to the third law. **For every action, there is an equal** (equivalent) **and opposite reaction** (or response). It means that as we push on an object, the object also pushes back. If we were to pull on an object, the object would also pull us towards itself. We are both exerting some kind of force between each other.

Imagine yourself in a small fishing boat and a friend is in a similar boat next to you. Neither of your boats are anchored, the water is calm and both of your boats are about the same size. There are no restrictions holding either one of the boats. If you were close enough to reach out and push (or exert force) on your friend's boat with your hand in an attempt to move away from him or her, what happens? Both boats move out of their current position away from each other.

Now picture your friend's boat being about 10 to 15 feet away from you and your boat. You are holding a rope that is attached to his or her boat. If you were to pull (exert force) on the rope in an attempt to get closer to your friend, what happens? Which boat actually moves from its current position, yours or your friends? Both boats move inward towards each other in the water. They pull on each other.

Astronauts in outer space, orbiting the Earth, are continuously falling towards the Earth along with the objects around them in the space capsule. They do not reach the Earth because the Earth is round and bending away from them, at the same rate as they are falling towards it. They would have to accelerate (or increase their speed of motion) towards the Earth in order to eventually reach the Earth.

Astronauts cannot move around very well in the capsule. Unless they have access to an object that they can pull or push up against; they have a difficult time trying to move out of their present state of motion. Astronauts push on an object such as a wall to propel themselves in the other direction. They apply force (or activate a temporary accelerating energy) against the direction that the wall is actually traveling in space. As the Astronaut pushes on the wall that is moving, the moving wall pushes back to continue its forward movement in space.

We have discussed the first and third law. Now let's look at the second law which is expressed in the formula, "Force equals Mass times Acceleration." A good example of this law in action is in picturing a childhood toy that some of us are familiar with. It is made up of a wooden paddle, a small rubbery ball and a long rubber band string about 1 foot long. One end of the string is attached to the paddle and the other end to the ball. Let's pretend that the rubber band string represents the force (push or pull) between the paddle and the ball. If you were to stand in one spot and spin yourself around in a circle while holding the paddle, the ball would begin to lift into the air and pull away from you and the paddle. The stretching of the rubber band indicates that a greater force has been activated (when applying a faster movement of motion). If you were to keep it spinning at a certain speed, the ball would stay pretty much in that orbit. If you were to spin a little faster or accelerate, the ball would pull farther and farther away from you, stretching the rubber band even more. A stronger force would be activated. This experiment is an example of how force and acceleration are related. According to

Newton's three laws, everything is moving, and everything pulls or pushes everything else.

We can change our present circumstances according to the three laws. God is the creator of these laws; Newton just discovered how they work. In order to make changes in our own lives for the better, we have to make a move. And, we have to trust God in that move. We in our own strength may not be strong enough to push obstacles out of our way. But, if we include God in our plans, He is bigger and more powerful than any obstacle standing in our way. We have to act on and **exert force** on what we want to change. It won't change by itself. We may come up against some resistance, but the more force we use the easier it becomes. If we don't, we will continue to exist in our same state.

Questions Chapter 6

1. According to Jesus, what is the key (4 letter word) that causes universal laws to go to work on our behalf? He said if we had _____ and doubted not, we could go as far as to command a mountain to be cast into the sea and it would obey.

2. Isaac Newton discovered three laws and we can change our present circumstance according to these laws. Which statement or statements would relate to taking the first step in activating faith to change our circumstances? Choose the correct answer or answers.

     A. Let our circumstances change by themselves

     B. We may come up against some resistance

     C. We will continue to exist in our same state

     D. We can change our present circumstances by exerting force on what we want to change

3. A _____ is the pull (attraction) between objects or it is the push (repulsion) between objects.

4. For every action there is an equal and opposite _____.

5. Everything is moving, and everything pulls or pushes everything else. Is this true or false?

6. The more force we use to change our circumstances, the easier it becomes. If we don't, we will _____ to exist in our same state.

PUTTING THE LAW OF FAITH INTO ACTION

---◆---

There are more interesting facts about these scientific laws and how they work for us in creating change in our lives. It may seem to be almost impossible to begin to create a dramatic change to achieve our dreams. But according to scientific principles, we can. I want to show that as we begin our step of faith, laws are activated that start altering atomic states and attracting the necessary components to bring about what we are hoping for. We can exercise faith by what we think, say and do, which in turn activates a force to pull good things toward us or repulse them away from us.

Isaac Newton's law of gravitation shows that when two objects are attracted to each other and they continue to draw towards each other, their force of attraction to each other gets stronger, and their speed towards each other continually increases.

As we reach out to achieve a goal, power is activated in the microscopic world of atoms to help bring it to pass into our lives. For every action we take, it can cause an equal reaction on the other side of the equation. **Hebrews 11:1 tells us that faith is the substance of things hoped for, and the evidence of things not seen.** I believe, that these laws can be used to show us how *we can attract into our lives the reality or actual manifestation of that which we are focused on* *and hoping for, natural or supernatural. The same law applies to both.*

Here are the three laws mentioned in the previous chapter.

1. Every object is in motion, and will remain in that state of motion until another external force is applied to it.

2. Force equals mass times acceleration. It is stated as an equation: $F = M \cdot A$.

3. For every action, there is an equal and opposite reaction.

Let's now look at Isaac Newton's Law of Gravitation. It is expressed in a formula.

$$((M_1 \times M_2) \times G) / R^2 = F$$

It basically means:

((Mass of 1st object x Mass of 2nd object) x G)

((Mass of 1st object x Mass of 2nd object) x G) {where G is a number that represents universal unchanging gravitational force} / **R^2**

{which is the distance between the center of two objects squared} **= Force**

Here are a few rules pertaining to the law of gravity. They may or may not help in understanding what the formula actually means. You do not need to understand the formula or the rules below. I will explain in more detail later.

Mass is the amount of matter an object is made of. Each one of us is made of a certain <u>number of atoms</u>, no matter where we are.

Mass is not the same as weight. Weight shows how much <u>gravitational pull</u> there is on an object. For example, the Earth is not perfectly round. It bulges around the equator and flattens at the poles. So the poles are closer to the center of the Earth. This means your weight would be slightly different depending on where you are standing.

Our weight on earth is different from what it would be on the moon. This is because the gravitational pull of the Earth and the Moon are different. The mass of the moon is smaller than the mass if the Earth. There are different variables that would have an effect on the situation. The distance between two objects is calculated from the center of both of their mass (center point of each object).

Distance squared in the formula means the distance is multiplied by itself. It is the distance times the distance between the two objects.

Force causes motion. Force can change the magnitude of movement and/or direction.

The **G** in the formula represents a number that is thought to be the same at all places at all times, and it shows the universal strength of gravitational force.

I am not a scientist or math major and there is so much more to these laws that I don't know. But in my research, I have learned enough of the basic concepts to believe that these scientific principles can show us how everything we do impacts the world around us.

I believe thoughts and ideas are real material substances. I can't tell you how much they weigh or their dimensions. But they exist because we can store them in our memory banks for later retrieval. Every thought we think is significant. The only thing that I am not sure of is how the **G** (gravitational constant) would relate to this system of thoughts.

$$((M_1 \times M_2) \times G) / R^2 = F$$

Let's use this formula to see how things could work in the faith world of thoughts. Let's say that the first object (M_1) is the image, idea or goal that you are thinking about. The second object (M_2) in the calculation is actual microscopic atomic elements that start coming together to make what you are hoping for a reality. Remember that according to the third law, when the first object pulls (attracts, pursues or moves forward), the second object or objects also pulls (attracts, pursues or moves forward) from the opposite side of the equation in the direction of the first object. For example, we have two magnetic bars with positive and negative ends. If you were to place the two bars facing each other negative to negative, they would repel each other. On the other hand, if you were to place the two bars facing each other positive side to negative side, the negative side would attract the positive particles to itself. For every action, there is an equal and opposite reaction.

Keep in mind what I said earlier regarding Hebrews 11:1. It tells us that , "faith equals the substance of things hoped for and the evidence of things not seen".

In this formula, M^1 could represent the faith substance of things hoped for, and M^2 could represent the actual substances or physical evidence of things you don't have yet or see yet with the natural eye. Faith is the sum of both sides of the equation just as it is in the scripture when acted upon. The law of attraction shows us that _our thoughts and actions can attract what is equal (the reality of the image that we are focused on and hoping for) and opposite (don't already have or see yet in our physical realm)._ Even though it may seem hard at first to change an undesirable circumstance into a desirable one, we can take action to cause a positive reaction. And, as things progress, it becomes easier to reach our goal. Things start coming together for us in ways that we never before thought possible. If Jesus said we can have life more abundantly, then we can.

This next section briefly explains how this attracting faith or fear force operates. If you are not interested in the detailed study, you may skip to SECTION B.

SECTION A

To see how this law can work for us, let's add some simple made-up numbers to the formula for example purposes. The mass of the 1st object (our faith or fear thought) is 300, mass of 2nd object (microscopic physical evidence) is 300, the gravitational constant is 10, and at some point in time once faith is activate, the distance between the two is 60.

$$((M_1 \times M_2) \times G) / R^2 = F$$
$$((300 \times 300) \times 10) / (60 \times 60) = F$$
$$(90,000 \times 10) / (3600) = F$$
$$900,000 / 3600 = \text{Force of } 250$$

When the number for the distance between the 2 objects is 60, the force between the two is 250. As the two masses draw near or attract to each other over time, their distance would become less and less. So using the formula, let's calculate again using 30 or half of the original distance of 60.

$$((M_1 \times M_2) \times G) / R^2 = F$$
$$((300 \times 300) \times 10) / (30 \times 30) = F$$
$$(90,000 \times 10) / (900) = F$$
$$900,000 / 900 = \text{Force of } 1,000$$

The force (attraction, pull or power) between the 2 items has increased even more and is now 1,000. It is 4 times stronger than when we began the formula. So the objects are now moving even faster towards each other because of the more powerful force (or pull).

We can use the second law, the law of motion, if we wanted to find out how much they accelerated towards each other.

(M x A = F)

(Mass x Acceleration = Force)

If we know the total Mass and the Force we

can calculate the Acceleration.

(F / M = A)

(Force / Mass = Acceleration)

Step 1. To find the Acceleration we would take the force that we got for each of the distances (first 60 and then 30), and divide them by the total combined mass (M) of the two objects. In the original formula, the total combined mass of M^1 and M^2 was 90,000. At a distance of 60 the force was 250. At a decreased distance of just 30, the force became stronger and increased to 1,000.

At a distance of 60

Force / Mass = Acceleration

250 / 90,000 = 0.00277778

At a distance of 30

Force / Mass = Acceleration

1,000 / 90,000 = 0.01111111

Step 2. Next, we subtract the acceleration amount calculated for the distance of 60 from the acceleration amount calculated for the shorter distance of 30. This will give us the **difference in speed** between the two as they continue to attract to each other. Acceleration is a change in an objects motion. It is the rate of change in velocity in a given amount of time or frame of reference.

A at distance of 30 **minus** **A** at distance of 60

(0.01111111 - 0.00277778 =0.00833333)

Step 3. Then, we divide this increase of 0.00833333 by the **A**cceleration amount calculated from the beginning distance of 60, which was 0.00277778.

(0.00833333 / 0.00277778 = 2.9999964)

An iIncrease of almost 3 times.

This step shows us that as the distance between the two masses decrease, the force and acceleration both increase. This means that the more the two masses pursue each other, the quicker and easier the pursuit becomes.

Imagine getting on a freeway entrance at just about 25 MPH and having to accelerate to reach a speed of 70 MPH. You would have to push the acceleration pedal with more FORCE to increases your speed. You could reach your destination a lot faster than 25 MPH as long as you did not crash, or there were no road blocks. The more you push to reach your destination, the closer you get to it!

Here is another really deep thought to the faith principle. What if M^2 starts with a tiny faith powered particle (like a seed) of some kind? Then, all the substances needed to grow M^2 would begin to attract or draw closer to each other, from all kinds of sources to form the ending results as the power of faith goes to work. It would seem to me that as particles begin to join together to form an ending result, their accumulating combined masses would become larger and larger numbers.

For example, if you wanted to start up a business from scratch, you would think it through first, and begin the process to get it going. You would need to get a building, supplies, employees, etc. As time goes by, you could eventually expand into a bigger company. Its mass would become a larger number. My thought in the formula is that if the mass number increases significantly, so does the force. In other words, as things continue to come together, the force would get even more powerful, accelerating the whole process, as long as nothing gets in the way to block its progress.

SECTION B

Hebrews 11:1 "Faith is the substance of things hoped for AND the evidence of things not seen". Every action of faith causes some kind of reaction. If there is no action, there is no faith substance to work with, and without faith substance there will be no evidence.

We can attract or repulse by what we think, say and do. We need to activate faith laws to bring into our lives what we need from God and to push away what we don't. A way to describe the word "attract" is to catch the attention of or invite, while the word "repulse" is to resist, force away, or fight off.

God is our source! He is a real being with feelings! To be connected with God is to be connected to life and all of its benefits. Instead of seeking things, seek the maker. We can attract or repulse God by what we think say and do.

In Exodus, Chapter 32, God's people offended Him by creating their own god out of jewelry. They had Aaron (their High Priest) form a golden calf, so they could worship it as their own god. God was so angry that He wanted to destroy them, but Moses interceded on their behalf. Later, God's people got their focus back on Him and willingly gave up some of their gold, silver, bronze and/or other items as an offering to help build His temple (Exodus 35:20).

We are mortal beings and do not always have the full knowledge and wisdom to know how to make things happen. But God does! Matthew 6:33 tells us that the key is to seek first the kingdom of God and His righteousness and all the things we need will be added into our lives. In fact, all of Matthew, chapters 6 and 7 tell us that He is our source and power. In Matthew 10:39 Jesus said, "He that

findeth his life shall lose it, and he that loseth his life for my sake <u>shall find it</u>."
Who's life is he referring to? He is referring to yours and mine. If we give up our self-centered way of living life for his sake, who's life will we find? The answer is that we will find our own life that God meant for us to have. It is the abundant life you and I were meant to have.

There is another formula that is similar to the law of gravitation. It is called Coulomb's Law. French Physicist, Charles Augustan de Coulomb's formula uses charges of energy represented by Q (for quantity charge) and R (radius or distance between them squared) in the equation instead of M (for mass) in the gravitational law calculation. It may be a more realistic formula choice since energy would seem to relate more to the power of thoughts and other things that we can't see.

$$((Q_1 \times Q_2) \times k_e) / R^2 = F$$

$$((1^{st} Q \times 2^{nd} Q) \times k_e / \text{radius squared} = \text{Force.}$$

$$k_e \text{ is electrostatic constant}$$

The difference that I want to point out between Coulomb's law and Newton's law is that Coulomb's law can represent an attraction (pull) or repulsion (push) between two energy charged objects, particles or things, whereas, Newton's law deals with the attraction (or pull) between two objects. So, either one of these formulas give us an idea of how universal law affects everything around us.

I am not a mathematician, and do not understand physics very well. But I do believe that they can help to explain how faith operates in this world. God is the designer and mathematician who makes all things new (Revelation 21:1-5).

Hebrew 11:1,"Faith is the substance of things hoped for, and the evidence of things not seen"

Let's look at Hebrews 11:1 as a faith formula:

((<u>Things hoped for</u> X <u>evidence of things not seen</u>) X <u>unlimited power of God</u>) / <u>our faith and trust in God</u>.

As we continue our journey to trust and expect God to fulfill our request with the evidence hoped for, the distance between what we are hoping for and the evidence itself gets shorter and shorter until it becomes a reality.

In summarizing the laws, when two objects or charges of energy get closer to each other, their attraction to each other becomes stronger and they move quicker towards each other. This means that as we pursue a more successful lifestyle (or something we don't already have), it becomes easier to obtain, as long as we continue our pursuit of what God knows to be best for us.

The down side of all this is that the process works the other way too. If we already have what we are focusing on, then our present circumstances cannot change. If we continue to pursue something that is not healthy for us, or we are not satisfied with, it will continue to happen.

We are in control and have spiritual and natural laws that operate to either help or hurt us. It all depends on our actions.

Questions Chapter 7

1. A force is the pull (attraction) between objects or it is the push (repulsion) between objects. Are we subject to these laws, yes, or no?

2. As we begin are step of faith, laws are activated that alter atomic states and attract the necessary components that brings what we are _____ for?

3. We can _____ (pull towards us) or we can repulse (resist and force back) by what we think, say and do. We need to exercise more faith energy to bring into our lives what we need from God and to push away what we don't from Satan.

4. According to the laws mentioned in the chapter, as we continue to pursue a goal, it becomes easier to obtain as long as we continue our pursuit. Is this true or false?

5. If we continue to pursue something that is not good for us, what will happen?

6. Things are going to turn out bad or good depending on our actions. Do you think we can alter our own destiny according to the laws involving force?

7. Hebrew 11:1-3 (NKJV) begins with, "Now faith is the substance of things hoped..." Could faith be associated with the force power in the formulas? Is Faith a real substance?

FOCUS CAN MAKE THE DIFFERENCE

---◆---

What we allow ourselves to think can become a reality. If we focus on the thoughts that we do not want or like, even if we don't want to focus on them, we can still draw or attract their equivalent to us without even realizing it. It is part of the cause and effect rule. For example, let's take thoughts of fear or worry. I said earlier that thoughts could come from the spiritual realm that we can't see or hear with our natural senses. When we listen to and focus on these thoughts, we increase or magnify the strength of their affect and attract more of the same. In other words, if we concentrate on fear or worry, we can attract more things that cause us to fear or worry.

One way to take control of the situation is to treat any negative thought as if someone were standing beside you and harassing you. Think of it as words not coming from your own self, but from another separate being. You don't have to listen. Remember that in the book of Matthew, Chapter 16, this is exactly what Jesus did when He turned to Peter and said, "Get behind me, Satan." He did not accept the words that Peter spoke to Him because He knew that the source was Satan. Satan gave the thoughts to Peter, and Peter spoke what was on his mind. Jesus knew that Satan attacks by influencing thoughts.

If you listen to a spirit of fear or worry, you are giving in to that spirit instead of fighting back or ignoring him. He will bully you as long as he knows you're listening. There is a way to fight back and put the enemy on the run. You must deal with the problem by changing what you focus or concentrate on. Use the laws that are established by God, that deal with repulsion and attraction to change your way of thinking. Block the thought from coming to you.

II Timothy 1:7 (NKJV) says, "For God hath not given us a spirit of fear; but of power, and of love, and of a sound mind."

The first step is to take the focus off of what you don't want. Prevent or block offensive and annoying thoughts with another thought. It will cancel out the affect of the negative thought. This interferes with and blocks the attracting forces of the harassing enemy. The more determined and forceful you are, the easier it gets. If you have ever had the experience of pushing a broken-down car off to the side of the road, you know that the hardest part of the push was when you first started pushing. But once you got the car rolling, it became easier and easier, almost going by itself.

In Gods Word, James 4:7 states that if you resist (which means to withstand and not accept) the devil, he will flee. If you recognize him and get the mindset to get rid of him, you can.

Create the new positive image in your head and use it to block what you don't want and create what you do want. I want to remind you again that **Hebrews 11:1 tells us, faith is the substance of things hoped for and the evidence of things not seen.** The laws of attraction show that you can attract what is equal (the reality of the image that you are focused on and hoping for) and opposite (what you don't already have or see yet in the physical realm). The Bible says faith is a real substance, we just can't see it with the natural eye.

We can expect great changes as we pursue them through God. It can happen according to proven scientific principles. Let's take healing, for example. The Bible tells us that healing has been provided for us through Jesus. It means any kind of healing ranging from disease to oppression and depression. The Bible tells us that we can even be healed from a broken-heart. If you need healing, start imagining yourself healed and press forward to a more abundant life. Create an image of wholeness in your thought life, and don't let go of it. Speak to yourself the words that tell you that it's yours. Input the right stuff and act on it. How can you receive healing, if your focus is always on the impossibility of it happening? If your faith seems weak and you are having a hard time believing healing is for you, ask God to show you in the Bible. Then, search for stories on healing. He loves you, and if He loves you, He wants the best for you. You do not have to suffer, Jesus did it for you.

> In Luke 4:18 (NKJV) Jesus said, "The Spirit of the Lord is upon me, because He has anointed me to preach the gospel to the poor; He has sent me to heal the brokenhearted, to proclaim liberty to the captives and recovery of sight to the blind, to set at liberty those who are oppressed."

When your focus is on the right stuff (like good health) and you reach out to God, you increase or magnify his strength in your own life.

Questions Chapter 8

1. If we concentrate on fear or worry, we can attract more things that cause
_____ or _____.

2. Satan attacks us by influencing _____.

3. How do you block a thought you do not want? Choose the best answer.

A. Take the focus off of what you don't want with another thought
B. Beg God to take it away
C. Beg Satan to leave you alone
D. None of the above

4. According to this book, the laws of attraction show that you can attract what is equal (which is the reality of the image that you are focused on and hoping for) and _____ (which is what you don't already have or see yet in the physical realm).

5. The Bible says faith is a real _____.

6. If your faith seems weak and you are having a hard time believing healing is for you, what can you do? Ask God to show you in the Bible and then _____ stories on healing.

7. When your _____ is on the right stuff (like healing) and you reach out to God, you increase (attract) or magnify his strength in your own life.

GIVE GOD THE REMOTE CONTROL

In my earlier years as a young adult, I had the misfortune of dealing with depression. I was continually tormented with negative thoughts. After I came back to God and accepted his Son, Jesus Christ, as my savior, his Holy Spirit helped me in finding ways of fighting back the enemy who had me bound by fear. One of the first things that I learned was that I could minimize an anxiety attack of the enemy by pre-occupying myself with something else. I would force other positive thoughts into my head. I would start reading healthy faith building material, or get busy occupying myself with a task.

Then, one day, as I was praying about the situation, I asked God about it. I asked the question, "What is the easiest, safest and best thought that I could force myself to think or say to counteract this state of mind?" The Spirit of God impressed to me the answer. It was simply this, "Why don't you think or say the phrase, Praise the Lord!" It had a four-fold purpose. It was a phrase that I could use to overlay the negative thoughts. It was a safe and positive thought. It would attract or magnify the presence of God, and if there were any evil spirits harassing me, they would not stick around to have a chat of how good God was. They have feelings, and they fear the presence of God.

James 2:19 (KJV) says, "Thou believest that there is one God: thou doest well. The devils also believe, and tremble."

So as needed, I would just repeat the phrase over and over again to myself. If I felt that a negative thought was getting stronger and starting to overwhelm me, then I would get louder and more aggressive with my positive thought. I was determined to beat this thing and was tired of it controlling my life. I was beginning to learn how to fight back, push my way through the enemy attacks, and stand on the promises of God that were in the bible.

Satan wants to be in control and attacks us through our thought life. God's Word tells us that our weapons of warfare destroy strong holds of the enemy. We are to reject imaginations and everything that exalts itself against the things of God. We can capture thoughts and surrender them to Christ by focusing in on God and giving Him control.

2 Corinthians 10:4-5 states, "For the weapons of our warfare are not carnal, but mighty through God to the pulling down of strong holds, casting down imaginations, and every high thing that exalteth itself against the knowledge of God, and bringing into captivity every thought to the obedience of Christ."

Think of thoughts as an internal television set with a remote control. We can pick what we want to tune into by changing the channel. Your TV set can be controlled by you, Satan or God. It depends on who has the remote control. Who is pushing your buttons? What channels are you tuned in to? If you don't like what you see and hear, then you can change it. It's your TV! Take the remote control away from Satan! Change your channel of thought by talking to God, meditating in his Word and praising Him.

James 4:7-8 (KJV) says, "Submit yourselves therefore to God. Resist the devil, and he will flee from you. Draw nigh (near) to God, and He will draw nig (near) to you."

THE WALLS OF JERICHO

There is a wonderful story in the Bible of where Gods people defeated a whole city in an unusual way. God gave them the script ahead of time that told them how the episode would end once they played it out. They were to march around the city of Jericho one time, each day for seven days. On the seventh day, they were to go around seven times and on the seventh time around, they were to let out a great shout, then take the city. Their obedience in doing what God said to do brought them victory over their enemy.

Joshua 6:20 (KJV) says, "So the people shouted when the priests blew with the trumpets; and it came to pass, when the people heard the sound of the trumpet, and the people shouted with a great shout, that the wall fell down flat, so that the people went up into the city, every man straight before him, and they took the city."

They followed God's script. They marched around the city whether they felt like it or not. They also shouted rather they felt like it or not. Feelings had nothing to do with it.

Romans 6:13 says to yield your self as an instrument of God. Yielding your body to praising God especially when the Devil tries to stir up bad feelings to make you feel defeated, can teach you how to take control back and win the battle. When you praise God you are blocking the thoughts from the enemy and forcing thoughts of God in your mind. You are changing the channel in your head's television.

There have been times when I felt it very difficult to reach out to God while praying. I felt like there was some kind of wall between us. I would ask myself, "What's wrong with me? Why don't I feel you God? Why don't I feel like talking to you? I would end up giving into my feelings and stop trying, even though I needed Him. Instead, I needed to ask myself the question, "How can I overcome and

55

overpower this feeling?" The answer was that I had to do just that. I had to overcome my feeling of not wanting to, by taking control and doing it anyway. In other words, <u>I had to give Him praise as if I already had the victory</u>.

Another reason that it may seem difficult to communicate with God could be unconfessed sin. Unforgiveness could be the only thing blocking or interfering with your prayers getting through. Ask for forgiveness if you need it and confess unforgiveness if you need to forgive someone else, and by all means forgive yourself. Do it without hesitation, rather you feel like it or not. Keep the communication line clear of any obstacles. Don't give the enemy a monkey wrench to throw in the way to stop your blessing. Forgiving is an act of Love. It is something you can take action and do. Faith works by Love.

The Word says to yield your body as a living sacrifice to God. Make it do what it should. Give God the attention He deserves by using your whole body. Reach out to Him with uplifted arms of surrender or on your knees in reverenced respect and honor. Or, if your in a situation where you are limited on what you can do like driving on the freeway, commune with Him by singing or speaking to Him. Music can be very therapeutic. Most worship songs talk of comfort, faith, peace and love. They are for your own benefit. You can take control and alter the state of your feelings. Yielding to God is a way of getting in tune with Him and training your physical body, your feelings and thoughts to obey you. You are blocking or canceling the negative influences that can affect you, and replacing them with the positive influences of God. Remember that the laws show as we exert force to pursue something, we are drawing towards whatever we are pursuing, and it in turn draws towards us. We are exerting force that attracts the good things of God to us.

Don't shout praises of joy only when you feel like it. Shout, applaud and praise God because He is worthy to rule and reign over us, and that you are looking forward to his coming where we will have total peace and joy with a perfect world system. There will be no debt, no crime, no hatred, no murder, no more war or suffering. Thank Him for carrying out a plan that made forgiveness and salvation available to us, and for loving us and being merciful. Thank Him for all your blessings! Thank Him that He hears your prayers! He can take care of a loved one's need when you can't help them yourself, because he can be everywhere at the same time. There are a number of reasons to praise Him.

God inhabits the praises of his people. We should praise Him whether we feel like it or not. We should act on faith, not on feeling. **Faith is** what we start with and it **is the real substance of things hoped for.** When we praise the Lord, we are magnifying his power and presence in us, because He is in us. Praise strengthens us!

So, in praising God, we are activating or working within the laws of attraction and attracting Him more and more into our life. When our thoughts and actions pursue our creator, He pursues us. It is drawing on his sources to change our circumstances.

He deserves our praise. Be thankful for your eyesight, hearing, and your ability to walk and talk. Thank Him for the roof over your head, food and clothing. Think of what your life would be like if you didn't have these things. You might appreciate having them a little more.

Psalms 100:4 (NKJV) tells us, "Enter into his gates with thanksgiving and into his courts with praise: be thankful unto Him, and bless his name."

We can rewrite the script for our lives as many times as we need to. We have the right and ability. As a little girl, I remember having nightmares of monsters and scary looking creatures chasing me. I would wake up terrified! Since then, I have learned that I don't have to be afraid. I don't have to be afraid, not because there is no such thing, but because I have Jesus. The Bible tells us that evil spirit beings are real. God has given me protection and power over the scary enemies like in my childhood dreams. When I occasionally have a similar dream now, it ends up different. I remind myself that they are scared of me because I have Jesus. So in my dream I would cast them out, or beat them up till they run away like a wiped puppy. Thank God I learned the truth! The idea is to remind ourselves who we are in Christ Jesus.

Jesus said, "Behold, I give unto you power to tread on serpents and scorpions, and over all the power of the enemy, and nothing shall by any means hurt you."

I would like to share a little tip that I made up that had worked for me in quickly blocking out bad thoughts. For example, there were times when I would be thinking about an upcoming event that was important to me, and I would begin to worry about how it would turn out. I would be thinking deeply about it, and would begin to imagine the worse happening in that event. So, I created my own way of dealing with the negative thought. As soon as I would realize what I was doing, I would block the thought with another thought. I blocked it by creating a thought of hearing a loud buzzer sound in my head. You know, like the one's you hear on game shows when the contestant would give a wrong answer. It may seem silly, but it worked for me in quickly stopping the thoughts from continuing in the wrong direction.

Is there anything that has you bound into a negative thought pattern? Is there something that keeps you in a defeated state of mind all the time? Do you keep mulling it over and over, again and again? Rewrite your own script. It is okay to think of all possible things that could go wrong as long as you plan out a positive reaction that you could take for each one. It may take practice and you may not always get the exact results you want. But, as you practice you gain experience. Take thoughts and use your God given authority and imagination to alter the story in your head to one of victory for yourself.

Philippians 4:8, Finally, brethren, whatever things are true, whatever things are noble, whatever things are just, whatever things are pure, whatever things are lovely, whatever things are of good report, if there is any virtue and if there is anything praiseworthy—meditate on these things.

Questions Chapter 9

1. What was the four-fold purpose of the phrase, "Praise the Lord"

A. It was a phrase to _____ the negative thought

B. It was a _____ and positive thought

C. It would _____ or magnify the presence of God

D. _____ _____ would not stick around to have a chat of how good God was

2. How do we know evil spirits have thoughts & feelings according to James 2:19?

3. What does 2 Corinthians 10:4-5 tell us regarding our weapons of warfare?

4. James 4:7-8, tells us to submit (draw, attract, force our attention or focus) to God and resist (push away) the devil. Draw nigh (near) to God, and He will draw nigh (near) to you." Is this law or action similar to Newton's law of attraction or Coulombs law of energy found in chapter 6 regarding universal law?

5. What should you do when you don't feel like reaching out to God when you need to? Take control and _____ it anyway.

6. Can unconfessed sin like unforgiveness block your prayers and/or your blessing?

7. Forgiving is an act of Love. Faith works by _____.

8. God inhabits the praises of his people. We _____ the power and presence of God into our own lives when we give him praise. The answer also means enlarge, expand, amplify and increase.

FOCUS ON WHAT YOU WANT THINGS TO BE

Force your focus on the end results that you want to accomplish. For instance, let's say that you're a smoker and you want to quit smoking. You smoke what you think is your last one and say, "Okay that's it, I am through smoking." A few hours later, you feel the urge for one coming on. You start imagining yourself taking that puff. It keeps taunting you. Your imagination is stronger than your will power. If you don't take control and change that image in your head, it will probably cause you to give in. Your focus has got to change!

What thoughts are you focusing on? Are they thoughts that help you quit, or ones that tempt you into wanting another? You can't say you're quitting and think about how good it would be to have just one more. Imagination wins over the will, so change what is in your imagination.

Just after I gave my life to Jesus, smoking was one of the things that, for myself, I did give up. As I sought God, He began to deal with me on certain issues. My view on the things going on in my life began to change. He gave me a desire to start cleaning up my life and one of the first things was to stop smoking. I began to think about how expensive they were. I could smell the odor on my clothes. I noticed my yellowing teeth and fingers, and I had a bad smokers cough. I could barely climb a flight of stairs without coughing or running out of breath. I burned a hole in my favorite dress and that was it for me. I was determined to give them up.

It was not a pleasant image to me anymore. The general idea of the story was that my focus changed. Instead of the image of how good they tasted, I thought of how they controlled me and caused problems in my life. I did not like them anymore.

As we draw our focus more on God, we draw from Him his healing power for ourselves. Years ago, I had hurt my back, and for months I could not turn my head to the left without intense pain. One day, I was sitting in a church service listening to the minister preach his sermon. As he was talking of how good God was, I began to ponder that thought very deeply. I was thinking of how good He had been to me. How He helped me with my depression. How so many times when I had been distressed, miraculous and mysterious little things would happen. I was thinking about the many times when fear had tried to overwhelm my thought life. I would open my bible to get my mind on other things, and to find something comforting to read. My eyes fell on the perfect words that I needed for that moment. They would be bright and bold as if to stand out on the page to catch my attention. I was also pondering other times when someone would quote a scripture or say the right words, as if God was right there talking through them to comfort me. I had a deep realization that God was here for me all the time and I hadn't even acknowledged his presence. I was thinking of how good He was and came to the realization that I really, truly liked Him, and not just because I needed Him! I appreciated Him! I liked his character and personality, and was thankful to have Him as my best friend. I liked who He was! As I was in deep thought, imagining all these things, all of a sudden, I felt this wonderful warm tingling sensation in my back. It felt so good. I turned to my mother to tell her that something was happening to my back, and realized that I could turn my head with no pain. At the same instant, the minister stopped in the middle of his sermon and said that someone just received healing in his or her back and neck. I knew he was talking about me and it was a wonderful feeling! God healed me even though I hadn't asked for the healing.

After that incident, I decided to study healing in more detail. I had heard that God heals only if He wills to heal you. As I studied the Word, I found that it was and is his will for every one of us. It was and still is available to every one of us, even today.

My point is that my focus was on God and his goodness. He is our source! God draws toward us as we draw toward Him! He will reveal himself to us if we seek him! Think about the people around you, if you praise and compliment them, they in turn like being in your presence, so they stick around. But if you murmur and complain, you drive them away. I hope I am not the only person guilty of this, am I? We should practice focusing on the right things. I am talking to myself here too. God is the source of all healing. If we please Him and show Him our appreciation, He in turn wants to please and prosper us in all areas of our lives.

God is pleased when we believe and take Him at his word, but He is angered when we don't. The story of Joshua and Caleb in Numbers, Chapters 13 and 14, is a good lesson for us all. This event happened about 40 years before the story that I mentioned in the previous chapter regarding the city of Jericho. It is the story of where God told Moses to send a total of twelve men (a man from each tribe of Israel) to spy out the land of Canaan. God told Moses that He would give them this land for themselves. It was described as a fruitful and beautiful land of plenty. But the problem was that the people that lived in the land of Canaan were giants compared to the Israelites. When the spies came back from spying out the land, there were only two of the twelve men, Joshua and Caleb who were convinced that if God said He would get it for them, He would. They were ready to go! The other ten men focused on how big their enemy the giants were. So they gave a bad report to the rest of the people. They convinced the people that the giants would defeat them. They caused the people to doubt God's ability. The people began to murmur and complain against God. They looked to their own strength to have to conquer the land and not how big and powerful their God was.

The reality of the situation was that their enemies were the ones that were like little tiny grasshoppers compared to their massive God. But they didn't see or imagine it that way. They had the wrong focus. Their unbelief displeased God so much that He said they would not be allowed to enter the land of Canaan at all.

The ten spies that gave a bad report all ended up dying of a plaque. The rest of the Israelite people wandered in the wilderness for forty years until the last of the unbelieving adults died off. Joshua, Caleb and all the children were the only ones that could still receive this promise. But they had to wait forty years. After the 40 years of wandering in the wilderness, Joshua had become the leader that led the victory march around the walls of Jericho. He had the right focus. He trusted in God, so God made him a leader.

Questions Chapter 10

1. Force your focus on the ending _____ that you want to accomplish by changing the negative image in your head.

2. According to the story of the 12 spies who were sent to spy out the land of the giants in Numbers, Chapter 13 and 14, did God respond disapprovingly to the Israelites that doubted Him at his word?

3. Did those Israelites focus on what they wanted things to be or where they intimated by the enemy that they saw in the natural? In other words, what was blocking them from pursuing their dream of living in the promised land?

4. In reality, who was more like little grasshoppers, the giants or the people of God, and tell why?

5. Which is bigger God or our problems?

6. Joshua had the right _____, so God made him a leader.

7. According to the story of the 12 spies, is it important to trust God no matter how things look in the natural? Is this true or false?

8. God wanted to bless the Israelites by giving them a beautiful and prosperous new land. The author claimed that she received healing even though she did not ask for it. Does God sometimes give more than what we expect or ask of Him? Before you answer the question, consider five bible stories listed next.

A. Consider the story in Acts 3:2-10. It was a story about a disabled man who was begging for money at the gate of the temple. Peter and John (disciples of Jesus) spoke words of healing to the disabled man and he was instantly healed. If you read the story, it does not say that he asked for healing. Did he expect to be healed? Verse 5 tells us he was waiting and expecting Peter and John to give him money. He was in the perfect frame of mind for receiving his healing because he had no doubt that he was going to receive something. Does that sound like faith? The only difference was that he just thought it was money. Peter and John had no doubt that the man would receive his healing and told the man to rise up and walk. The man received something much better than a little money to buy his next meal. He was made completely whole. God sees and honors those who trust in Him like Peter and John.

B. Acts 16:25-26, is where Paul and Silas were put in prison for preaching. The Bible tells us that they began singing praises to God while they were in prison, and suddenly there was an earthquake, the prison doors were opened and everyone's chains were loose. Was that a coincidence?

C.1 Kings 19:1-8, Elijah, the prophet of God came to a point in his life where he became weary and cried out to God to let him die. He wanted to give up. God sent an angel to bring him food for strength. The Bible says he was able to go in the strength of that food for 40 days and 40 nights.

D. Daniel 3: 17-28 is the story of Shadrach, Meshach and Abednego who were cast into a fiery furnace by the King because of their faith. They trusted God with their lives and God honored their faith. The Bible tells us that when they were thrown into the fiery furnace, the King saw a fourth man walking around in the furnace with them and they were all unhurt by the fire. The three men came out of the fire and in verse 30, they ended up getting promoted in their jobs.

E. 1 Kings 3:5 is the story where God told young King Solomon to ask for anything he wanted. The only thing that King Solomon asked for was wisdom to rule his people. God was so pleased with his unselfish request that He gave King Solomon his request and in verse 13 God told him He was also giving him riches and honor.

Does God sometimes give more than what we expect or ask of Him, yes or no?

TIME AND ETERNITY

———— ◆ ————

Jesus is real and is alive today! He is still performing miracles! In the natural thinking, this statement seems unrealistic. We don't physically see Jesus walking around, giving speeches, laying his hands on sick people or doing all the works He was known for in the Bible. What we do see concerning Jesus, is other men and women physically carrying on his works in his place.

If we could go behind the curtain of the drama called life here on Earth, we could see that it is possible for Jesus to still exist as a real person. In a live performance, there is a lot of activity that takes place back stage that we don't see or even think about, to make the show a success. Could Jesus exist as a real person after all this time? It would seem unbelievable, or is it? I believe that Jesus is alive and immortal, and performing from behind the scenes in a dimension unseen with the naked eye.

Scientific studies have been done to show that there could be a state of existence where time is at a standstill. This dimension of existence is at the speed of light. Light is the fastest phenomenon in the universe that we know of. Its maximum speed is 186,000 miles per second in a vacuum and it slows down when it travels through substance. It is capable of traveling 7½ times around the world in one second. It is very fast compared to sound. We know this by seeing the crackle from the lightning and hearing the thunder seconds later. They both happen at the same time, but the light travels faster than the sound.

Albert Einstein believed that time slows down as it approaches the speed of light, and it stops completely at the speed of light. Time is a system we use to measure the advancement of events and it has everything to do with motion.

Einstein's theory has been tested using atomic clocks. There is detailed information about the clock experiment on the internet. The clocks were taken on commercial flights around the world at about 600 MPH, then compared to clocks that were stationary on the ground. As the jet traveled eastbound the time on the clocks were less and when they traveled westbound the time on the clocks were more by nano-seconds. If the high-speed trip affected the time on the clocks, it also should have had the same affect on the people involved by this same theory. I wonder how it would have affected them if it were possible for them to have traveled at closer to the speed of light. How would it affect their aging process?

Years ago, I made a video recording for a scene in a church play. It was based on 1 thessalonians 4:16 through 18 regarding the coming back of the Lord. Scripture says that we will be caught up to meet him in the air. The play was based on these scriptures. The scene I was recording was about a man (let's call Dave) sitting in a chair talking to his brother (let's call Bob) sitting on a couch. After a few minutes into their conversation and before Bob could bat an eye, Dave disappeared into thin air, leaving his clothes behind in the chair.

In order to create the scene, I sat the video recorder down in a stationary position and began recording Dave sitting in a chair talking to Bob. I then put the recorder on pause to suspend its time frame for a few minutes. Dave got up from his chair, went into another room, changed into another set of clothes and positioned his original clothes in the chair that he had been sitting. Then he went back into the other room to hide. He stayed there for the duration of the filming. I then started up the recorder again so that in the next frame it looked like he instantly disappeared out of his clothes. In reality, the clothes incident took place between the 2 time frames (or events of time) recorded. But, if you were to view the video, you would not see anything happening in between the time that it took Bob to shut his eyes in the first frame and open them again in the second. When you watched the video to see the drama unfold, you didn't see how Dave disappeared. In the film, from Bob's perspective, Dave disappeared at closer to the speed of light. Dave was able to step out of the time frame and do what he did while Bob was at a standstill. The whole event took 15 minutes, while the actual recorded time was 10 minutes. For Dave, time was slowed down to a standstill long enough for him to complete his task of changing clothes and hide before the next time frame. Jesus, like Dave in the story is not affected or limited by time as we know it. He dwells in the light of eternity.

This scene reminds me of a Star Trek episode, were Captain Kirk had been slipped a drug in his coffee by some alien being. The drug caused him to exist in an accelerated state of being. His crew could not see him, but he could see them moving very slowly. They were moving so slowly to him that he could move from one side of the room to the other before they could bat an eye. Events in time around him elapsed very slowly.

Think of a moving sidewalk inside of an Airport. While you walk on it, it moves along by itself to speed up your movement. It helps you get to your destination gate faster. If you had a friend who was going with you on a trip and he or she decided to walk on their own without taking the moving sidewalk, it would take him/her more time and effort to get to the destination gate than it would you. He or she would move at a much slower pace. You would have time to get a snack, take a restroom break or do something else before your friend finally catches up to you. The moving sidewalk would have helped you get more done than your friend in less time.

You may be wondering by now, how is this all related to Jesus? Scientific research shows that if it were possible for one of us to be able to exist and move about at closer to the speed of light in our own dimension here on Earth, we could age at a much slower pace. If it were possible for one of us to move at closer to the speed of light and exist in our own time frame, just think of how much we could get done in less time. To others, we would be moving so fast that they could not see the changes taking place. It would seem instant. A good modern day example of this is with a television or computer screen. The images are redrawn so fast that we can't see the actual images being drawn. If this is true, then through Gods Spirit, molecular changes can occur in what seems to be instantaneously to us. Jesus could move closer to the speed of light in (another dimensional time frame, at will) between our slower time frames without us seeing Him. He could alter substances before we could bat an eye. This study shows that there could be a state of existence the Bible calls eternity and that changes can occur instantly without us seeing them happen. It also tells us that Jesus could be alive and live for all eternity.

As time goes by, our bodies will age and die. When we die, our spirit will not be able to live in our physical body made up of atoms. Genesis 2:7 tells us that God formed man out of the dust of the ground. He then breathed into his nostrils the breath of life and man became a living soul. When Adam and Eve sinned, God told them in Genesis 3:19 that they would return to where they came from, which was the ground. Later, Adam and Eve had two sons, Cain and Abel. Genesis 4:8 shows that Cain killed his brother Abel. In verse 10, God confronted Cain and said, "What have you done? The voice of your brother's blood crieth unto me from the ground." Even though Abel was dead in the natural body, he still existed. Our bodies may die and be returned to the ground but our spirit will still exist.

Jesus is alive in his resurrected body and will never die again. He never ceased to exist even though his body became lifeless at his earthly death. The Bible says that at his death, He (the man inside the body) descended into Hell, but was not left there.

Acts 2: 31-32 (KJV), "His soul was not left in hell, neither did his flesh see corruption. This Jesus hath God raised up, whereof we are all witnesses."

God, through his Holy Spirit raised Him from the dead, healed and restored life to His body, and since He already paid the price of death, death could not contain Him ever again.

In Luke 24:39 (NIV) Jesus said, Look at my hands and my feet. It is I myself! Touch me and see, a ghost does not have flesh and bones, as you see I have." He was made immortal, a perfect, incorruptible man who will never age. There were many witnesses that saw and spoke with Him after his resurrection and before He ascended to Heaven.

Acts 1:9-11 (KJV) And when He had spoken these things, while they beheld, He was taken up; and a cloud received Him out of their sight. And while they looked stedfastly toward Heaven as He went up, behold two men stood by them in white apparel; which also said, Ye men of Galilee, why stand ye gazing up into Heaven? This same Jesus, which is taken up from you into Heaven, shall so come in like manner as ye have seen Him go into Heaven.

1 Timothy 6:14-16 (NIV) talks about the future appearing of Jesus Christ. Verse 15 and 16 says,: … in his time He shall show, who is the blessed and only Potentate, the King of kings and Lord of lords. Who only hath **immortality, dwelling in the light** which no man can approach…"

2 Peter 3:8 tells us that one day is with the Lord as a thousand years, and a thousand years as one day.
I believe eternity has everything to do with the speed of light. Jesus can step in and out of our realm of existence. He is not restricted by our hours, minutes, seconds or timing of events. He can be everywhere and anywhere. He can live and have his being in us, if we let Him. He is alive and working with us to complete his mission. Acts 1:11 tells us that He will be back in his earthly body.

Mark 16:15-20 says, "And He said unto them, 'Go ye into all the world, and preach the gospel to every creature. He that believeth and is baptized shall be saved; but he that believeth not shall be damned. And these signs shall follow them that believe; In my name, shall they cast out devils; they shall speak with new tongues; They shall take up serpents; and if they drink any deadly thing, it shall not hurt them; they shall lay hands on the sick, and they shall recover.' So then after the Lord had spoken unto them, He was received up into heaven, and sat on the right hand of God. And they went forth, and preached everywhere, the Lord working with them, and confirming the Word with signs following. Amen."

Questions Chapter 11

1. Time is a system to measure advancement of events and has everything to do with motion. Albert Einstein believed that time slows down as it approaches the speed of _____. Scientific studies have been done to show that there could be a state of existence where time is at a standstill. It is at the speed of _____.

2. In the clock experiment, the high-speed trip going east (with the rotation of the Earth) showed that the time on the clocks were slower than the clocks sitting on the ground. Would it have the same effect on the people who went on the trip with the clocks? In other words, could they have aged at a slightly slower rate than the people with the stationary clocks on the ground?

3. When people die, they cease to exist. Is this true or false?

4. According to scripture, Jesus was brought back to life. People saw Him and spoke to Him after his resurrection. Was there other evidence of Him in his own physical body? What was the evidence?

5. If Jesus is now an eternal being, He would not physically_____ as we do?

6. If He could move about at the speed of light, could He multi-task in the time it takes us to blink an eye, yes, or no?

7. After Jesus ascended into Heaven, Mark 16:20 says, "And they went forth, and preached everywhere, the Lord working with them, and _____ the word with signs following."

8. If Jesus dwells in the light, is an eternal being, and to Him one day is like a thousand years, can He still be performing according to Mark 16:20, yes, or no?

GOD'S SON

Jesus was a remarkable man. He had power to raise the dead, heal the sick, cast out devils, walk on water and He was able to live a total sinless life. He was God's own Son and was sent to re-unite us with God.

He said in John 10:10, "The thief cometh not, but for to steal, and to kill, and to destroy: <u>I am come that they might have life, and that they might have it more abundantly</u>." John 10:28-30 "And <u>I give unto them eternal life</u>; and they shall never perish, neither shall any man pluck them out of my hand. My Father, which gave them me, is greater than all; and no man is able to pluck them out of my Father's hand. I and my Father are one."

The first man, Adam sinned against God and activated the law of sin and death.

Gen 3:17-19, God said, "Because you listened to your wife and ate from the tree about which I commanded you, 'You must not eat of it,' Cursed is the ground because of you; through painful toil you will eat of it all the days of your life. It will produce thorns and thistles for you, and you will eat the plants of the field. By the sweat of your brow, you will eat your food until you return to the ground, since from it you were taken; for dust you are and to dust you will return."

God basically said, "Adam, look what you have done. You caused a curse for yourself and it will be passed down throughout all of mankind." God did not do it, Adam did. God had to fix what Adam did. There was nothing Adam could do, at this point. So God had to fix it himself. And, He did it through his own Son, Jesus.

The universal law that proves for every action there is a reaction is prevalent in this case. The action of Adams' disobedience led to the reaction of eternal death for all of mankind and the action of Jesus and his obedience led to the reaction of eternal life for all of mankind. We can cancel the negative forces that lead to a life of destruction and pursue a life of abundance. The faith force has already been activated by the action of Jesus and the reaction is an eternal life of abundance for anyone who chooses to accept what he did.

All the accounts of Jesus in the bible tell us that there was something different about Him. The Bible tells us that He was born of a virgin, and that He was not conceived in the natural way as the rest of us. His father was not an earthly man. You could say that his genealogy was different on his Father's side of the family.

DNA (Deoxyribonucleic acid) is what ensures that living organisms produce their kind. Molecular genetics is the study of how information can be passed from one generation to another by genes. For example, physical traits such as what a person looks like, their hair or eye color and facial features are all passed on to us by our parents. The down side of this is that genetic disorders such as heart disease and cancer can also be passed on by the genes.

A gene is a very long, thread-like structure made up of DNA. DNA include the hereditary characteristics located in each cell of our bodies. The information is stored using four chemicals (adenine, cytosine, guanine, and thymine). Each of these chemical structures is paired up with one of the others in a series of rows. The different combinations of the chemical bases represent coded information passed down from previous generations.

The very long thread-like gene of DNA is coiled tightly together many times in the shape of an X or a Y. This X or Y shaped mass of DNA is called a chromosome. Chromosomes are passed on from the father and mother to the child.

The top half of the child's X chromosome comes from the mother and the bottom half of the child's X chromosome comes from the father or vice versa. So the X chromosome is made up of the DNA from each parent.

Each one of our cells normally contain twenty-three pairs of chromosomes. Twenty-two of these pairs look the same in men and woman (X shaped). The twenty-third pair of chromosomes is called the sex chromosomes. The female's sex pair of chromosomes are both X shaped, whereas the male's sex pair chromosomes have an X shaped chromosome and a Y shape chromosome. Women do not normally carry the Y chromosome. The Y chromosome is the only one that has male dominating features. So the father's Y chromosome would be what would determine if a newborn child were to be a male. Jesus was a male child, so the sex chromosome would have had to come from the father's side of the family not the mother.

The bible tells us that Jesus was conceived by the Holy Spirit of God. So God was his Father, and some features were passed down to Him from God. Artificial fertilization technology was not around back in the time of Jesus, but it is today. We now know that it is possible to implant what is needed from the father into the mother to create an embryo without the sexual experience. If his Father was God, then He had characteristics of his Father. He was the first born of a new lineage.

As for having the unique DNA passed on from his Father, (making Him a descendent of God), He had supernatural creative powers and abilities like his Father. The human side of Him from his mother, Mary (a descendent of Adam) was able to have access to those supernatural creative powers and abilities, because He was both God and mankind.

Part of the God nature in Him was that He was able to live a sinless life. He was put to death by mankind in the prime of his life even though He had a right to continue living. He did nothing wrong worthy of death. He paid a price He did not owe. His spirit and soul were driven from his body when He was crucified.

Isaiah 53 (NLT), "Who has believed our message? To whom has the Lord revealed his powerful arm? My servant grew up in the Lord's presence like a tender green shoot, like a root in dry ground. There was nothing beautiful or majestic about his appearance, nothing to attract us to Him. He was despised and rejected— a man of sorrows, acquainted with deepest grief. We turned our backs on Him and looked the other way. He was despised, and we did not care.

Yet it was our weaknesses He carried; it was our sorrows that weighed Him down. And we thought his troubles were a punishment from God, a punishment for his own sins! But He was pierced for our rebellion, crushed for our sins. He was beaten so we could be whole. He was whipped so we could be healed. All of us, like sheep, have strayed away. We have left God's paths to follow our own. Yet the Lord laid on Him the sins of us all. He was oppressed and treated harshly, yet He never said a word. He was led like a lamb to the slaughter. And as a sheep is silent before the shearers, He did not open his mouth. Unjustly condemned, He was led away.

No one cared that He died without descendants, that his life was cut short in midstream. But He was struck down for the rebellion of my people. He had done no wrong and had never deceived anyone. But He was buried like a criminal; He was put in a rich man's grave. But it was the Lord's good plan to crush Him and cause Him grief. Yet when his life is made an offering for sin, He will have many descendants.

He will enjoy a long life, and the Lord's good plan will prosper in his hands. When He sees all that is accomplished by his anguish, He will be satisfied. And because of his experience, my righteous servant will make it possible for many to be counted righteous, for He will bear all their sins. I will give Him the honors of a victorious soldier, because He exposed himself to death. He was counted among the rebels. He bore the sins of many and interceded for rebels."

The best part of all this is that the LIFE, the God nature, the spiritual DNA that is in Christ, is what He wants to share with us as a gift. We could not go back in the past and physically give Jesus his life back in his own body, even though we (mankind) owed it back to Him. But God can, and did! We can let Christ live, by letting Him live through each one of us in our own bodies. We can let God's new spirit-born nature live in us. If we do, then we will also become descendants of God the Father. Jesus was the first born. And through Him we can become sons and daughters too. We must be born again!

Questions Chapter 12

1. Who, through the power of God, raised the dead, healed the sick, cast out devils, walked on water, had a successful career with many followers and lived a sinless life? Choose the correct answer.

A. Jesus   B. Paul   C. Moses   D. Adam
E. None of the above   F. All of the above

2. John 3:15 reads, "Whosoever believeth in Him should not perish, but have eternal life." Jesus died for everyone, so everyone is automatically safe from eternal death, even those who reject Him. Is this true or false?

3. ADAM activated the law that puts us in RIGHT standing with God. Is this true or false?

4. Could Jesus have been born of Mary only? Why or why not? The answer has to do with X and Y chromosomes.

5. Begotten means born of God. According to John 3:16, "For God so loved the world, that He gave his only begotten Son, that whosoever believeth in Him should not perish, but have everlasting life." According to this scripture, could DNA of Jesus be from the heavenly Father, God?

6. John 3:17 reads, "For God sent not his Son into the world to condemn the world; but that the world through Him might be saved." Jesus came to fulfill the death penalty once and for all by giving his own life. What do you think fulfill means? Choose the best answer.

A. Adams action caused a reaction in the laws that govern our universe. Jesus produced another action that caused a reaction in the laws that govern our universe. Jesus paid the price for the crime.

B. Jesus was sent to condemn and carry out the death sentence on ALL of Adam's descendants.

C. None of the above

7. Jesus did not have any children to pass on his inheritance from his Father. In regards to the gift from God, do you think we can inherit some of the same faith characteristics (the God side of DNA) that Jesus had? Remember, God was able to first implant his nature (as the baby Jesus) in Mary. Is He capable of imparting this nature into us?

THEIR PLAN

The universal law, "action causes reaction" originated from God. The law shows that when one object pursues the other, the other pursues back. As each one exerts more effort, so does the other. And, they can eventually unite with each other. Every action and every word that God did or spoke with his people up until the time of Jesus, and all the things said and done by Jesus while living on Earth, set into motion (or established) new and better conditions we can live by. Jesus became the doorway to the Father and to eternal life.

In the Old Testament, whenever God's people killed an animal for food, they were commanded to pour out the blood on the ground and cover it with dust. It was not to be ingested. When animals were used for an offering to God in the Old Testament, the blood of the innocent animal was to be sprinkled on the altar. Innocent blood of animal sacrifices had a special meaning to God.

In Leviticus 17:11 (KJV) God said, "For the life of the flesh is in the blood; and I have given it to you upon the altar to make an atonement for your souls; for it is the blood that maketh an atonement for the soul."

Blood is the part of the body that brings life. The blood circulates to every living cell in the body to bring it nourishment and to carry-off the waste and toxins. The blood also has antibodies that fight and prevent infections and diseases. When the blood stops circulating, life ceases to exist within that body.

All of the animal sacrifices of the Old Testament were temporary solutions for the sin problem until the time of Jesus. In John 1:29, Jesus Christ is referred to as the Lamb of God that takes away the sins of the world. Jesus came willingly to fulfill and settle the death penalty that was set into motion by Adam once and for all. When Jesus was about to be crucified on the cross, He let everyone know that He could call on his Father and his Father would rescue Him. Jesus could have asked the Father to send angels to fight for Him and deliver Him from being put to death on the cross. One angel alone is capable of killing 185,000 men in one night according to Isaiah 37:36. He willingly gave his body to become the ultimate sacrifice to make amends for our sins. We cannot redeem ourselves and are indebted to Him. He bought the rights to our existence and if He had not done what He did, we would all perish.

In Matthew 26:53 (KJV) Jesus said, "Thinkest thou that I cannot now pray to my Father, and He shall presently give me more than twelve legions of angels?"

After Jesus died, He was resurrected. The law of sin and death could not hold Him because He had no sin. He ascended to the heavenly altar of God to present his own sinless and shed blood to the Father. If by one man's sinful life (Adam) the death sentence was in force, by another man's sinless life who was put to death, the death sentence was paid. Jesus is worthy to approach the Father and we can come to the Father through Him.

Hebrew 9:12 (NIV) says, "He did not enter by means of the blood of goats and calves; but He entered the most holy place once for all by **his own blood**, having obtained eternal redemption".
Verse 14 says, "How much more, then, will the **blood of Christ**, who through the eternal Spirit **offered himself** unblemished to God, cleanse our consciences from acts that lead to death, so that we may serve the living

God!"

John 3:16 (KJV) says, "For God so loved the world, that **He gave** his only begotten Son. That whosoever believeth in Him should not perish, but have everlasting life."

God in Heaven and Jesus while here on Earth in a human body both contributed to carrying out and completing a plan of redemption for us all. If you think about their plan, God knew what He wanted to do, so He supplied the lamb (substitute). Jesus knew what He had to do, so He became the lamb (substitute).

Between God the Father and Jesus the Son, they set out to change the present circumstances. They focused on and pursued their goal of canceling the effect of one law (the law of sin and death) and establishing another (the law of righteousness and faith). They created a new passageway between 2 different realms of existence, the earthly (temporary) and the heavenly (eternal) for us all. God (whose throne is in Heaven) in one realm, and Jesus (on Earth) in another, both worked in perfect cooperation to re-unite themselves to each other. Their purpose was to cause a deviation in the future destiny of mankind. They gave and pursued their goal until it happened.

Let's compare the things that God from Heaven and Jesus (as a man) here on Earth did to make the connection between God and man.

God - *Even though God had supernatural abilities to deliver his son from suffering on a cross, He did not. He loved us so much He was willing to let his son die.*
Jesus -*Even though He could have freed himself by asking God for an army of angels to deliver him, He did not. He loved us so much that He was willing to die.*

God - *He gave his only son, something that He loved so dearly.*
Jesus - *He chose to please his Father because He loved him so dearly.*

God - *He used supernatural abilities to help mankind. He gave by devoting his time to restoring mankind to himself. He backed up his son with signs and wonders needed to set people free and cause devils to flee.*

Jesus - *He used supernatural abilities to help mankind. He gave by devoting his life to restoring mankind to his Father. He backed up his Father with signs and wonders to set people free and cause devils to flee.*

God - *He supplied the atonement for us and then He accepted the atonement from us.*

Jesus - *He supplied the atonement by becoming the atonement that was supplied by God.*

It was a well-planned and continual process of reconciliation from the beginning of mankind's fall to re-unite mankind back to God. It was done through establishing words and actions. For example, Jesus completed his part of the action to fulfill and end the law of sin and death when He spoke the words, "It is finished!" He also established a new law to give us forgiveness when He said, "Father, forgive them for they know not what they do!" He asked the Father for forgiveness, and God the Father did the forgiving. By the actions that they both took separately (from two different realms, Heaven and Earth), but together as one, they completed one law, and established a new and better law (or covenant) between man and God. ***They made a new connection.***

There is more to their awesome story. Jesus (representing mankind) gave himself as the atonement when He said, "Father into thy hands I commend my Spirit!" I believe the saddest moment between God and Jesus was at the cross. At his last breadth, Jesus tells the world that He is giving his Spirit, his life into the trusting hands of his Father. Mankind had no idea that they were playing a part in an awesome plan of salvation. Jesus first descended into a compartment in Hell. While there, I believe because of the God part of his DNA and his sinless life He lived on Earth, He had the power to overturn Hell and set the captives free. The

84

law of sin and death could not hold Him!

I think that when it was all said and done, his Father was so proud and well pleased with Him for carrying out the plan. Jesus proved his deity, his love for mankind and honor to his Father. It took great faith in the face of fear. The other wonderful thing about the rest of the story is that God now has his Son back. I think it made Him a very happy God. Wouldn't you be if you were re-united with your child?

All of Heaven celebrates every time a soul is added to his kingdom because of Jesus and what He did. In Luke 15:10 Jesus said, ".There is joy in the presence of the angels of God over one sinner that repenteth."

The Father and the Son made a way where there seemed no way. Now it is up to us to apply the plan to our own lives. God wants to put this same Spirit that was in Christ in us. It's his gift to us. He created a cure that fixed what Adam did. It nullifies the curse in your life by giving you a brand new life. God wants us to be his sons and daughters.

Hebrew 9:15-18 (NIV) says, "For this reason Christ is the mediator of a new covenant, that those who are called may receive the promised eternal inheritance—now that He has died as a ransom to set them free from the sins committed under the first covenant.
In the case of a will, it's necessary to prove the death of the one who made it, because a will is in force only when somebody has died. It does not take effect while the one who made it is living. This is why even the first covenant was not put into effect without blood."

It was necessary for Jesus to die, in order for us to receive what was in his will. His written will is the Bible (the written Word of God). It tells us that we can have forgiveness, healing, freedom, prosperity and eternal life. We have a right to live a blessed life now and forever through Jesus Christ, our worthy king and leader. It is a gift for all of us. We just have to accept it by faith.

Questions Chapter 13

1. The law regarding action and reaction originated from God. The law shows that when one object pursues the other, the other pursues back. As each one exerts more effort, so does the other and they both eventually _____ with each other. The plan of God was to re-unite mankind to himself.

2. Life of the flesh is in the _____ and it has been given to us to make atonement for our souls.

3. Jesus knew He would die if He went through with the plan. He could have called angels to _____ Him.

4. Jesus willingly became the ultimate sacrifice that would pay the price (fulfill) and cancel the effect of the 1st law, the law of _____ and _____.

5. God (who is in Heaven) in one realm, and Jesus on (Earth) in another, both worked in perfect cooperation to _____ themselves to each other. This is the same answer as question number 1.

6. By the actions that they both took, the Father from _____ and Jesus (his Son) from _____, completed (or fulfilled) one law, and established a new and better law (or covenant) between man and God. They made a new and better connection.

7. Is there celebrating in Heaven? What is the celebration all about according to Luke 15:10?

8. Was there goal reached in affecting spiritual and/or universal laws?

9. When is a will in force?

10. Did Jesus leave us a will? Can we consider the Bible a will or contract from God?

THE INVISIBLE REALM

We are limited in our own physical bodies as to what we can accomplish by ourselves. We can't see everything there is to see or hear everything there is to hear in the physical realm. Our eyes and ears have limits. Just because we don't see or hear some things, doesn't mean they aren't there.

Earlier, I briefly mentioned cell phones. We don't hear all the conversation traveling through the air or all the music from different radio stations around the world, and it is probably a good thing that we don't. We need to use special equipment that can tune in to the right frequency that we wish to hear. With voice activation, we can now speak a command into the air while driving our automobiles and special equipment causes things to happen to carry out what we say.

Modern technology helps us do many wonderful things. If we can believe in wireless communication, like cell phones and the fact that there are millions of words traveling through the air all the time without us seeing it happen, why can't we believe that there are other sources of communication that we can't physically hear or see?

We not only have physical senses for communication, we also have spiritual senses or special equipment that can communicate with the unseen world. Even though we can't physically see or hear Satan or his evil counterparts, he still can and does send ideas and thoughts that we pick up on with our inner ears and eyes. On the other hand, there is also another source that can communicate with us through our spiritual senses. He is referred to as the Holy Spirit of God. We may not see or hear Him with our natural senses, but He is just as real as Satan, or other spirit beings such as angels and demons. They are all capable of communicating with us because we are also spirit beings. The difference is that we have a limited physical body and they don't.

We are in physical bodies and therefore have limitations. There are so many things that we can't see or hear that exist all around us. There are different levels of visible and invisible forms of energy that affect our lives everyday. The most visible type of energy is the light that we see. Light consists of energy in the form of electromagnetic fields.

Different colors that we see represent different frequencies of light energy. (A frequency measures the number of waves that pass a particular point per second). Red is the least amount of energy and is the longest wavelength that we can see. Violet has the most amount of energy and is the shortest wavelength that we can see. White is a combination of different colors that we see.

There are other energy level frequencies that we can't see, but by which we can be affected. They affect us in different ways.

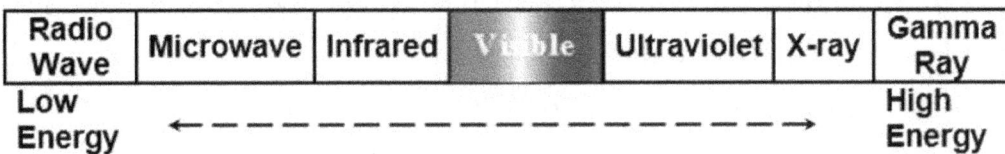

Radio Wave	Microwave	Infrared	Visible	Ultraviolet	X-ray	Gamma Ray

Low Energy ← – – – – – – – – – – – – – – – → High Energy

Radio wavelengths – have the least amount of energy. They pass through most things, even us. So, we can't see or hear them, but they are there.

X-ray wavelengths – have a high level of energy and pass through most things. They can pass through most of our body parts except our bones and teeth. Our bones and teeth are made up of larger atoms than the rest of our body, and their atomic energy level match closer to the energy level of the X-ray wavelength. X-rays can be dangerous because they can apply so much energy that they can knock an electron completely out of its orbit.

Gamma wavelengths – have the most energy of all. They can travel across the Universe. They also pass through things because of their extremely high energy level.

We believe things are going on around us even though we can't see them. As you read this book, radio waves are probably passing through your body right now without affecting you.

Even though we have limitations, there are advantages to being in a physical body. First of all, it is a barrier that gives us some protection from evil spirit beings. They can't just barge in and take over. They have to find loopholes. And in order for them to do their dirty work, they use pressure to manipulate one's thoughts into their way of thinking, so they can gain control of the persons physical actions.

The second advantage is that the Holy Spirit of God can dwell with us and help us live life to the fullest. We go by what we see and hear, and like the different types of light energy, there are other things out there rather we see them or not. A physical body does not limit the invisible Spirit of God. He can see and hear everything. He created it all! He sees all! He knows all! We need him for guidance because He knows things we don't.

Another advantage to having a physical body is that we can enjoy interacting with others and the things around us. We can enjoy life. We can enjoy the taste of food, hear birds sing, see God's majestic creation and feel God's love through others. All things were made for God's glory and enjoyment. He can enjoy the life of his creation through us.

Colossians 1:15-16 (KJV) is where Paul (the writer) is discussing Jesus. He says, "...who is the image of the invisible God, the firstborn of every creature." Verse 16 says, "For by him were all things created, that are in Heaven, and that are in Earth, visible and invisible, whether they be thrones, or dominions, or principalities, or powers: all things were created by him and for him."

Questions Chapter 14

1. Cell phones, radios and televisions are devices or special equipment that we use to see or hear something that we can't see or hear with the physical eye or ear alone. Is this true or false?

2. We may not see or hear the Holy Spirit with our natural senses, but He is just as real as Satan, or other spirit beings such as angels and demons. They are all capable of communicating with us because we are also spirit beings. The difference is that we have a limited physical _____ and they don't.

3. Can some light energy sources pass through our body, yes, or no?

4. Even though we can't see X-ray wavelengths with the natural eye they can be very dangerous to us. They can apply so much energy that they can knock an electron completely out of its orbit. Is this true or false?

5. Some energy wavelengths can travel across the _____.

6. Who does the chapter say is the image of the invisible God that created all things according to Colossians 1:15-16?

7. A physical body does not limit _____. He can see and hear everything and is given to us as a gift.

BY HIS SPIRIT

───────◆───────

Jesus tells us in John 1:12-13 and in John 3:1-7 that we must be born not of physical flesh and blood, but of God's Spirit. In other words, it is not automatic to be spiritually born and right with Him. There is something that we must do to receive the new birth, or new beginning. Romans 10:9-13 and 2 Corinthians 5:17-18 also tell us to be born again. The term "born again" has been referred to as being "saved" from a fallen state of being.

The first step in being born again is to acknowledge our fallen state and ask for forgiveness. We should ask ourselves if we measure up to God's perfect standards. Secondly, we must accept the death of Jesus as atonement (compensation or punishment) for our sins, and that he paid any price for our faults and inadequacies. We must accept that Jesus is the Son of God, and that He was raised from the dead. Through Jesus, we become adopted sons and daughters of God according to Romans 8:14-16. We become joint and rightful heirs with Jesus Chirst (the Son of God) to the promises of God. I believe our very DNA is affected by the result.

Romans 8:14-16 (NKJV), "For as many as are led by the Spirit of God, these are sons of God. For you did not receive the spirit of bondage again to fear; but you received the Spirit of adoption by whom we cry out, "Abba, Father!." The Spirit himself bears witness with our spirit that we are children of God, and if children, then heirs—heirs of God and joint heirs with Christ."

When Jesus died, He gave his Spirit into the hands of the Father so that the Father could give his Spirit to us. After his death and resurrection, He was seen and heard by many. Just before his ascension into Heaven, He mentions some things regarding the Holy Spirit (Ghost).

John 20:22 (NIV) tells us that He breathed on his disciples then said the words, "Receive the Holy Spirit! If you forgive anyone's sins, their sins are forgiven; if you do not forgive them, they are not forgiven" (This scripture says that Jesus delegated authority to the disciples to affect other peoples lives.)

In Luke 24:49 (NIV) it is recorded that Jesus also said, "I am going to send you what my Father has promised; but stay in the city until you have been clothed (or endued) with power from on high." (He told them that they would soon be receiving something else regarding the Holy Spirit from the Father. The word power in this scripture is the kind of power to reproduce itself. It is a creative power!)

Another thing that Jesus had said before his ascension into Heaven was, "John baptized with water, but in a few days, you will be baptized with the Holy Spirit" (Acts 1:5 (NIV).

After Jesus ascended into Heaven, Acts 2:1-8 tells of a very special and miraculous event that took place on a religious holiday called Pentecost. While they were all assembled together to give praise to God, a strange and awesome thing happened. In the middle of their praise service and as they were praising God, the words that they spoke came out in other languages that they themselves did not know.

Acts 2:4 reads, "And they were all <u>filled</u> with the Holy Ghost (Spirit), and began to speak with other tongues (languages), as the Spirit gave them utterance."

Acts 2:6-8 (KJV) reads, "Now when this was noised abroad, the multitude came together, and were confounded, because that every man heard them speak in his own language. And they were all amazed and marveled, saying one to another, Behold, are not all these which speak Galileans? And how hear we every man in our own tongue (language), wherein we were born?"

A little later, Apostle Paul explains to the Church the purpose of the Holy Spirit. He explained that the Holy Spirit was given to us to strengthen and help us through life. He becomes a part of us, knowing our deepest dreams, fears, hurts and wants. He is available to us with supernatural power and guidance to help us even when all else in the natural realm fails. Don't be afraid of the Holy Spirit! Trust him! He is our connection with the Father. He is the Father himself, who wants to and can be as close to us as our own heart.

Romans 8:26 (NIV) says, "In the same way, the Spirit helps us in our weakness, We do not know what we ought to pray for, but the Spirit himself intercedes for us with groans that words cannot express."

We not only need to be born of God's Spirit to help us in living our own lives, we need him to help us pray for our loved ones. They may be right in front of us or far away in another state or country. We are only human and have limitations. He does not! His Spirit can work where we can't. Our bodies do not limit him. He has access to all of the creative forces in the faith realm which is the unseen realm of existence.

Questions Chapter 15

1. Jesus said we must be _____ again, not of flesh and blood, but of the Spirit. The first step is to ask for forgiveness. We must accept the new covenant for ourselves by believing He is the Son of God and that He was raised from the dead.

2. If we are led by the Spirit of God then we are sons and daughters of God. If we are his children, we are then _____.

3. In Luke 24:49, Jesus told his followers that He would send the promise of the Father and that they were to wait in Jerusalem until they were endued with _____.

4. There was a supernatural event that took place in Acts 2:4-8 as the worshippers began praising God. They were filled with the Spirit of God and began to speak in a _____ that they themselves did not know.

5. The Holy Spirit is given to us to strengthen and _____ us through life. He is available to us with supernatural power and guidance to _____ even when all else in the natural realm fails.

6. From the last paragraph, name at least 3 characteristics of the Spirit of God?

7. The Spirit of God is all knowing and all powerful and can work where we _____.

JOY IN HIS PRESENCE

All things are possible through God. Everything we do in the present moment affects our future. Our journey and our destiny are determined by choices we make now. The most important decision that we will ever make is accepting Christ as savior. He is the way to a better life now and for eternity. Through trusting and believing in him, we can change our circumstances for the better.

Romans 10:17 tells us that faith comes by hearing the Word of God. Faith is a real substance of some kind, and is activated when we get into and stay focused on the Word of God. Just like focusing on fear or worry can attract things that make us fear or worry, focusing on faith thoughts attract things that cause us to activate more faith. We may not be able to see, hear or touch an actual tangible item called faith in the natural, but we can experience its results. God is a real being and God is love. Faith is power in action and it works properly by love.

Unlike emotions such as fear, worry and depression, faith is so powerful that it brings about healthy physical changes. It produces a real confidence and a knowing that all will be well. It relieves stress. It can turn tears of sadness into tears of joy. It rejuvenates and energizes the body and mind, and heightens ones resistance to sickness.

The Word tells us that we can receive healing through faith in God. If you study the first four books of the New Testament, you will find that Jesus tells us to believe. He healed people everywhere he went. Doctors help us in every way they can in the natural sense for healing. Thank God for doctors! We also have wonderful technology in the world today to help diagnose and heal. But sometimes it is not enough! Doctors can't see in the spiritual realm or at the microscopic, sub-atomic level where molecular changes could be taking place. Healing may start with a single component of an atom. Chemical property changes could be set in motion that they may not be able to see with the human eye, or with all the advanced technology that they already have. Maybe your miracle is on its way, and you just can't see it yet with the natural eye. It may take time to heal, or it might happen in a twinkling of an eye. Don't give up on your miracle!

Fill your heart and mind with faith things. Practice speaking words of faith and stop speaking words of unbelief. The Word of God tells us that words spoken are the difference between life and death. Be careful with words. Psalms 45:1 says, "...my **tongue is the pen** of a ready writer." The tongue can write what is said on the **tablet of our hearts**. Words can carry or transmit energy (or power). If the life we live and the words we speak are in harmony with the Word of God, the affect of our words can be so strong and forceful, that they can cause what we say to come to pass.

Voice activation technology is becoming a norm on many things of today. We can speak a command into the air while driving and voice activated equipment carries out what we say. Certain command phrases have been pre-programmed into its memory banks. We can speak into our cell phones or to our television sets. We can now turn lights on and off in our homes just by speaking the command.

As Christians, the Spirit of God resides within us. He is a real being, and He has a mind of his own separate from our own mind. When we speak God's Word for our own lives, we are causing or allowing him to speak through us, with us, and for us.

It is like the two of us are in agreement and speaking at the same time. We are activating the original words spoken and inspired by God. We are letting the Holy Spirit use our mouths to release his power, which is backed by all of Heaven and its angelic host.

In Matthew 18:18-19 (KJV) Jesus said, "Verily I say unto you, whatsoever ye shall bind on earth shall be bound in Heaven; and whatsoever ye shall loose on earth shall be loosed in Heaven. Again I say unto you, that if two of you shall agree on earth as touching any thing that they shall ask, it shall be done for them of my Father which is in Heaven."

In Matthew 18:20 (KJV) He also said, "For where two or three are gathered together in my name, there am I in the midst of them."

John 15:7 (KJV) He said, "If ye abide in me, and my words abide in you, ye shall ask what ye will, and it shall be done unto you."

Paul said in Romans 10:8 (NIV), "<u>The Word is nigh thee, even in thy mouth, and in the heart; that is the Word of faith,</u> which we preach."

In Matthew 21:21 (KJV) When Jesus cursed a fig tree that withered up and died, He said, "Verily I say unto you, if ye have faith and doubt not, ye shall not only do this which is done to the fig tree, but also if ye shall say unto this mountain, be thou removed, and be thou cast into the sea, it shall be done." In verse 22 He said, "And all things, whatsoever ye shall ask in prayer, believing, ye shall receive."

If I decide that I want to learn a new trade such as how to be a doctor, lawyer, pilot, truck driver, or carpenter, I would need to study all I could by reading, hearing and practicing. If I were to stick with it, I could eventually become very good at it. It takes time and effort. To be a Christian means to become more like Christ. It is a continual learning experience. We need to train ourselves to be careful what we say. What we say while interacting with others and what we say in our prayer life affect everything in and around us. Little things we do can make a difference.

Practice changing some of the everyday unproductive phrases or things that you say and do. Some examples of repetitive sayings are, "I just can't remember", "It can't be done", I can't afford it, or "Oh, that's just great", when it's not. When you catch yourself saying negative things, cancel them out with positive words. If you can catch yourself before you get ready to say them, don't say them at all. Practice saying what you really want to be true for your life.

Fill your heart, mind and mouth with faith things. Practice speaking words of faith and stop speaking words of unbelief. You can't have both activated at the same time.

As Christians, we are heirs of royalty because we are adopted into the family of God. Our Father owns it all. We need to learn to walk and talk like we belong. As children of God, we are not inferior. Satan is a liar and has been since the beginning of time when he convinced Eve that she was inferior.

In John 14:1-3 (KJV) Jesus said, "Let not your heart be troubled: ye believe in God, believe also in me. In my Father's house are many mansions: if it were not so, I would have told you. I go to prepare a place for you. And if I go and prepare a place for you, I will come again and receive you unto myself; that where I am, there ye may be also."

God is concerned for our well being. He knows we have needs in the here and now and He wants to meet them. Proverbs 3:6 reads, "In all thy ways acknowledge him and He shall direct thy paths". Matthew 6:33 Jesus said, "**Seek ye first the kingdom of God,** and his righteousness: and all these things shall be added unto you".

God is our provider and the Bible tells us that the key is to seek his kingdom. Your miracle may be on its way. Don't say or do things to cancel it out. Don't listen to or agree with Satan and his negative influence by speaking unbelief. Get into and stay in sync with the Word of God. When Jesus talked to others and when He prayed to his Heavenly Father, his words were always words of faith. Put your trust in God like Jesus did. Tell him that you are trusting him. Keep telling him until you believe it yourself.

Romans 14:17, "For the kingdom of God is not a matter of eating and drinking, but of righteousness, peace and joy in the Holy Spirit."

Psalms 16:11, Thou wilt shew (show) me the path of life: in thy presence is fullness of joy. At thy right hand there are pleasures for evermore.

There is joy in his presence. This can become a reality in each of our lives. Years ago, after I received Christ back into my life, I began to get involved in doing things in a local church. I developed a curiosity of who God was, how He acted, and why He did the things He did in the different stories of the Bible. As I read them, I would play the scenes in my imagination. I began to see how longsuffering He was and learned of his love, compassion and interest in his people.

The more I searched the bible, the more I learned to trust him. It eventually led to a breakthrough in my life. One day during the worship part of a church service, I became really focused on worshiping God. All of a sudden I began to feel such a great joy, so overwhelming that I did not want to contain myself. You would have thought that I had just won a million dollars. I got so excited that I began to shout praises to God. I did not care what others around me thought. The feeling was so tremendous! It didn't just affect me! Others were touched in the same way and joined me in the joy of praising God. I did not care if I died and went to Heaven at that moment. I thought, "If this is what it feels like to be in his presence, give it to me now." Nothing could have felt as good as the high that I felt at that moment. The effects of the experience stayed with me for months. My tears of sorrow turned into tears of joy. Everything else in life seemed so trivial. There is a true joy in his presence!

If the Spirit of Christ is in us, and we lift him up in praise and magnification, we are empowering him, as well as ourselves. We magnify, draw and strengthen him in our own being. We can have a little bit of Heaven here on Earth now. There will be a time when we will be in the full glorious peace and joy of the lord at his return to rule and reign as King of kings. He will establish a new and perfect kingdom of God world system.

Fight the good fight of faith and don't ever give up! Take on the challenges that you feel defeated in, and on purpose, do the opposite. God is the creator of life and Satan is the destroyer of life. If Satan has defeated you in any area of your life, it means that he knows you are capable of great things. His attacks are to keep you from fulling God's plan for your life.

If you have a fear of him, he has deceived you into believing a lie and he can wreck havoc in your life. But he also knows that if you realized the real truth about yourself, which is that Jesus gave you power over him, then he would fear you. You are capable of wreaking havoc for him.

All the laws that govern the universe were created and set into motion by God. Remember that we can attract and accomplish what we are hoping for because the Bible tells us we can. Scientific facts provide an answer on how faith can work for us, and it proves that we can accomplish what we are hoping for. Jesus is the doorway to the Father and He tells us to share the good news with others.

He said in Matthew 10: 7-8 (KJV), "And as ye go, preach, saying, the kingdom of Heaven is at hand. Heal the sick, cleanse the lepers, raise the dead, cast out devils; freely ye have received, freely give."

These words tell us that it is his will for us to have healing and freedom, and we can share it with others through the supernatural power of God. He said, ".the kingdom of Heaven is at hand." This means it is available now. What would be the point of him telling us to go and perform the same works that He did, if it wasn't God's will? There are so many things happening behind the scenes of life's drama that we can't see happening with our physical eye.

Faith is a principle of God that can work for anyone who puts it into action. But, Jesus said in Mathew 16:26 (NIV) "What good will it be for someone to gain the whole world, yet forfeit their soul? Or what can anyone give in exchange for their soul?"

102

In Mark 16:17,18 and 19 Jesus said, "And these SIGNS shall follow THEM THAT BELIEVE: In my name shall they cast out devils; they shall speak with new tongues; they shall take up serpents; and if they drink any deadly thing, it shall not hurt them; they shall lay hands on the sick, and they shall recover. So then after the Lord had spoken unto them, HE WAS RECEIVED UP INTO HEAVEN, and sat on the right hand of God."

Mark 16: 20, "And they went forth, and preached every where, the LORD WORKING WITH THEM and CONFIRMING THE WORD WITH SIGNS FOLLOWING."

This act of faith took place after Jesus rose from the dead and ascended up to the Father. He is our connection to the Father. He is the author and finisher of our FAITH according to Hebrews 2:2.

There is scientific evidence that proves all things are possible with God. Through the accomplishments of the Father, the Son and the Holy Spirit we can reach out and achieve great things. Their combined efforts and actions have already been activated and made accessible for us through Jesus Christ. We have a right to access the blessing and good things that come from God himself because we are forgiven, cleansed spiritually, and accepted as sons and daughters.

Jesus created a direct access line to our creator, who is as near to us as our own heart. We exercise faith when we give praises and honor to God. Neither sin nor the devil himself can keep us from our maker and Father. Praising God as our Father works for our benefit, just like repeating or quoting scripture does to inscribe them on our hearts.

Let's look at a few definitions for praising God.

When we say, "I praise you, Lord", what are we saying?

Praise in the online Wikipedia, Free Encyclopedia says that it is the act of making a positive statement about a person, object or idea and that it is an expression of gratitude.

When we say, "I magnify you, Lord", what are we saying?

Magnify or Magnification in the online Wikipedia Free Encyclopedia says that it is enlarging something in appearance to see more details.

We magnify him to increase his greatness, power and his importance in us.

When we say, "I worship you, Lord", what are we saying?

Worship in the online Wikipedia Free Encyclopedia says that it literally means "worth-ship" and it is giving worth to something

When we worship him, we are saying or causing our heart to love him. We are acting out our love for him.

We say these faith empowering words to bring him into our presence. It is an act of exercising faith. What about the words glorify, bless, exalt, adore, appreciate, awe or awesome? If we look up their meanings, we can get a better understanding of what we are doing when we give praises to God. He wants us to exercise our faith in praising him for our benefit. God inhabits (lives and exists in) the praises of his people. He needs something to inhabit in order to work his love.

Questions Chapter 16

1. It doesn't matter what choices we make because our future is set and we can't change our present circumstances? Is this true or false?

2. If we continue in the Word of God, it will help us with our faith. What part of the body is like a writing pen and what part is the tablet?

A. Nose and feet   B. Tongue and heart   C. Knee and elbow   D. Pen and paper

3. When we _____ Gods Word for our own lives, we are causing or allowing him to _____ through us, with us, and for us. It is the two of us _____. We are activating the original words spoken and inspired by God. We are letting the Holy Spirit use our mouth to release his power which is backed by all of Heaven and its angelic host.

4. Proverbs 3:6 reads, "In all the ways acknowledge him and He shall direct thy paths." What does He say to do in Matthew 6:33 in order to have our needs met?

5. Romans 14:17 reads, "For the Kingdom of God is not a matter of eating and drinking, but of righteousness, peace and _____ in the Holy Spirit."

6. Who does the chapter say you are a threat to?

7. Universal laws were created by God. Can we consider the law that says, "ACTION CAUSES REACTION", as a pattern or blueprint to taking a step of faith?

8. Can you think of at least two other words of praise to the Lord? Look up their definition and see if you can identify how they can benefit your own life. Some are found in the chapter.

IT IS NOT TO LATE

It is not too late to change our destiny. The truth is that everything in the Bible did and will happen if it already hasn't. The Bible tells us of things past, present and future. It foretells the outcome of our world.

The Bible shows us our need for Christ. This world system cannot make it without his divine leadership. Jesus has been given all power and authority by God. He has proven to the Father that He is worthy to rule our world.

While He was on the earth, He used the written Word to preach to and teach others. He never spoke against it. He always spoke in line with what it said. He referred back to the written Word throughout his ministry. He also spoke it as a weapon against Satan. Why does He go to such great lengths to show us how He valued the written Word? I believe it is because He is trying to reveal to us a very important lesson. He is telling us where our power comes from, which **is** the Word of God.

The Bible says that faith comes by hearing. When we read the Word to ourselves, we are applying it into our physical and/or spiritual ears. This faith substance, in turn gets embedded into our thoughts and spirit.

I said earlier that there is a spirit world that communicates with us. There are actual spirit beings carrying out activities based on the written Word. Angelic hosts are working behind the scenes to enforce the written Word that seals our future. The spirit world is very real, where good and evil forces are at war regarding our eternal lives. We are involved rather we like it or not.

The written Word is important to us because it is a way that God can directly communicate with us. Jesus depended on the written Word and he knew the power behind it. After all, He is the Word from God made in human form. The Word is a doorway to the spirit world. It is ALIVE! I pray you get a revelation of this statement, "It is the **LIVING** WORD OF GOD!" It can talk to us! It can warn us or comfort us or heal us. I know that sounds strange, but as we read It, it places a substance (like planting seed) inside of us that can affect and change our destiny.

One of the first books of the Bible that I read in my earlier years was the book of Revelation. It is a very hard-hitting and strange book. The first time that I read it, I was terrified by all the frightening things it warned me about that would happen on the Earth. Sometime later, and as I became to know Jesus Christ a little better, I decided to read it again. This time I saw a totally different side of the book. I saw the good that was to come for those who follow him. He is coming to put an end to evil and establish good forever. It will be a time where there is no more war, no more crime, no more tears, death or sorrow. It showed a peaceful time with an awesome and wise King who loves and cares for us forever. He was involved in the creation of our world. Therefore, He knows how to run the affairs of our world successfully.

There are two roads in life for us to take. One leads to destruction and the other is a road map to unlimited spiritual treasures. Which path we choose is up to each one of us. Our action now will cause a reaction in our own future destiny. God sets before the world blessing and cursing, or life and death. It is not too late for us to change the destiny of our World. If only the World would heed the warning and lay hold on God's way of running things. It is not too late.

Deuteronomy 30:19, "I call Heaven and Earth as witnesses today against you, that I have set before you, **life** and death, blessing and cursing; therefore, **choose life**, that both you **and your descendants** may live."
Proverbs 10:22, "The blessing of the LORD makes one rich, and He adds no sorrow with it."

Isaiah 43:25, "I, even I, am He who blots out your transgressions for my own sake; and I will not remember your sins. Put me in remembrance; let us contend together; state your case, that you may be acquitted (found not guilty).

Deuteronomy 28:1-2, "Now it shall come to pass, if you diligently obey the voice of the LORD your God, to observe carefully all His commandments which I command you today, that the LORD your God will set you high above all nations of the earth. And all these blessings shall come upon you and overtake you, because you obey the voice of the LORD your God."

In Matthew 22:37-40 Jesus said, "You shall love the Lord your God with all your heart, with all your soul, and with all your mind. This is the first and great commandment. And the second is like it. You shall love your neighbor as yourself. On these two commandments hang all the Laws and the Prophets."

Isaiah 54:17, "No weapon formed against you shall prosper...."

Revelation 22:17, And the Spirit and the bride say, "Come!" And let him who hears say, "Come!" And let him who thirsts come. Whoever desires, let him take the water of life freely.

Hebrews 11:1 reads, "Now faith is the substance of things hoped for, the evidence of things not seen." Think about this scripture and define faith in your own words. Can we change our own destiny? Can we change the destiny of the World?

Chapter 17
Bonus Question

1. Hebrews 11:1 reads, "Now faith is the substance of things hoped for, the evidence of things not seen." Think about this scripture and define faith in your own words. Can we change our own destiny? Can we change the destiny of the World?

Please note: Answers to questions are at the end of this book after more tips.

FAITH THOUGHTS AND TIPS

Begin to change what you can change right now. Take control of what you can. Instead of complaining about a bad situation, talk and act like the desired result is coming. Activate your faith! Do all the things that you know to do to get it and help others to do the same! Help them to also activate the laws and principles that God set before us for good things to happen!

1 John 5:15 (KJV) says, "And if we know that He hears us, whatsoever we ask, we know that we have the petitions that we desired of him." A petition is a (formal, written or verbal) request to an authority. See what the written Word says regarding what you need and talk to God about it.

Start praising God for the answer. We are told to enter his presence with praise and thanksgiving. Think of things for which to be thankful for. Start somewhere, even if it's a small thing. Thank God for everything you do have.

Confuse opposing thoughts by speaking into yourself good thought. De-activate their stronghold on your natural man.

Study the Bible. John 5:39 (KJV) says, "Search the scriptures; for in them ye think ye have eternal life: and they are they which testify of me."

> Faith comes by hearing the Word of God. Studying the Bible activates faith and helps in overcoming doubt. Learn it, memorize it and speak it back to yourself. Feed on it.
>
> Learn and get to know God's character, his likes and dislikes and of his great love, mercy and grace.
>
> The Bible is the gateway to eternal life.

The Bible is a weapon against principalities and powers of darkness because it is the inspired written Word of God. We can speak the Word against our enemy and say it is written.

The Word is alive. It heals, sets free and causes supernatural miracles.

We can say, "It is written." Affirmations do not have to be presently true. It is not a lie to confess the Word of God as your own. It is creating the circumstances that you desire in your life and getting your life to line up with the "Word of God" (Bible).

Develop and define your goals, beliefs and values. Force yourself to think out a plan for your life if you don't already have one. Don't let things just happen. Find out what you can contribute to the world. What is or will be your mark in life? There are many resources on goal setting that are free on the Internet.

Words have power to change. Say it and pray it whether you feel like it or not. Speak words of victory and conquest, and not of defeat. Call things that are not as though they are. Give God permission to act on your behalf. For example, you are not automatically saved. You have to confess yourself as a sinner and ask for forgiveness.

After you ask the Lord to forgive you, forgive yourself. He forgives and forgets. As a child of God, you are standing in the righteousness of Jesus, not your own.

Take note of the thoughts that are annoying you. Write them down, so you can sort out what you feel. Then, find scripture that supports what you want the situation to be. Pray it and say it to yourself. Brainwash yourself with the Word. The more you work on memorizing it, the more you convince yourself it is true and the less you will believe the annoying lies of the enemy.

Cast down negative imaginations and create new ones. If you know it's the enemy, get mad at him and imagine him as a wimp. Whatever the imagination is, change it to one of victory. Use your imagination for your benefit. That's why we have one! Take authority of your thoughts! Change the image to one of success. Athletes picture themselves defeating their opponent before the actual event. They practice over and over again.

You are more than a conqueror through Jesus Christ. All power is given to him and He has made it available to us. Devils fear Jesus! John 1:12 reads; "But as many as received him, to them gave He power to become the sons of God, even to them that believe on his name." James 2:19 tells us that Devils believe and tremble. Look at your problems as a challenge. Some people like competition. After I got saved I gained more courage by stepping out on faith. Things that had before restricted me from enjoying a normal, healthy lifestyle became victorious adventures. After a while I gladly took them on. It became a spiritual high for me when I would win the battle. I was beginning to feel more self-confidence and to know the meaning of the thrill of victory.

Take care of your body. Exercise, eat right, and take vitamins if you need to. Stress can take a toll on the body. When I went through depression, I had a number of health problems because of it. I had ulcers, low blood sugar, poor appetite, and heart palpitations. I remember that my doctor gave me vitamin B shots once a week for a while and I would feel some immediate relief. Remember that the Word of God does good like a medicine too! Take it like you would take a prescription medicine. As we read the Word, it begins to give spiritual, emotional or physical healing. And, it strengthens our faith and gives us confidence to live a wonderful, full life again.

Love others! Love is an action. Jesus said the greatest commandment was to love God. The second commandment was to love your neighbor as yourself. Look for ways to add value to the world we live in. <u>If we want love then we need to give it.</u> <u>Whatever you need, give it. Like things attract like things.</u>

Strive for positive feelings. Anger can make you sick and usually does not carry any rewards and neither does worry. If the emotion is non-productive, talk yourself out of it. Find reason why you should let it go. Reason with yourself. If it seems hard to stop hurtful or negative feelings, write them out on paper. Get them out of your head. Release them, then throw the paper away as a symbol of release or counteract them with speaking, hearing and seeing scriptures that remedy the problem every time you need to.

Make time for prayer. Jesus wants to be your best friend. Talk to him. He is a real person. You just can't see him. Included him in everything you do.

Pray through his Holy Spirit. In Jude 20 Apostle Paul tells us we build ourselves up on our most holy faith, by praying in the Holy Ghost.

Let the Spirit of God speak through you and to you to strengthen your inner man. As you do, He will give you the power that you need to accomplish great things in life.

Be willing to take a stand and don't give up. Encourage yourself and give it time. Jesus compares his kingdom of righteousness, joy and peace to a grain of mustard seed that can grow into a mighty tree.

As far as healing, He has already provided healing. You can take it by faith. There are numerous healing stories in the Bible that took place before and after Jesus ascended to Heaven. His followers performed the supernatural works that He did. Reading them will build faith to receive healing for you and for those for whom you pray and intercede.

John 14:12 (KJV) says, "He that believeth on me, the works that I do shall he do also; and greater works than these shall he do; because I go unto my Father."

Matthew 8:5-13 (KJV) is a story of a Roman Captain that came to Jesus to ask him to heal one of his servants. Jesus told him that He would. The Roman Captain understood Jesus' authority and believed that all Jesus had to do was to speak the word of healing and that his servant would be healed. He believed that Jesus did not have to physically be there for the healing to take place. Jesus said, "I have not found so great faith, no not in Israel." Then He said, "Go thy way, and as thou hast believed, so be it done unto thee." The bible said that the servant was healed that very hour.

All things are possible through God and you can do all things through Christ Jesus who strengthens you.

PRAYER

If you have not made the decision to make Jesus Christ your Lord and Savior, you may do so now with this simple prayer.

Prayer

Almighty God of Heaven and Earth, I come before you to ask for forgiveness for any of my wrong-doing, in any way. I admit that I am lost without you and need you in my life. Please forgive me of all and any of my sinfulness. I invite you into my life. Please, heal me, deliver me and set me free! I pray your will to be done in my life as you renew a right spirit in me. Teach me and guide me. I give to you all my hurt, bitterness, anger, that has happened as a result from others or that I caused myself. I confess forgiveness to all those who have hurt me, even if I don't feel like it. I speak it as a reality in my life.

I ask to be born again of your Spirit to give me new life. Please, give me a brand new start! I confess Jesus Christ is the Son of God, who died for me, paying the price for my sinfulness. I receive and confess you into my life. I speak and take this new life by faith. I thank you for receiving me into your kingdom and coming into my heart. I am now going to be okay because I trust you with my life. I know I am not perfected yet. As I make mistakes, please forgive me and help me to get back on track. Thank You Holy Spirit for your redeeming power. Thank you Jesus for redeeming me. Thank you Heavenly Father for becoming my Father and accepting me into your family. In the name of Jesus I confess and pray!

Amen.

You can also inform your biggest enemy, that there has been a change in plans. He is no longer in charge because Jesus has set you free.

Devil, I choose now to belong to Jesus, not you. I refuse to go down with you. From this moment on, Jesus is my lord and savior and you have no right or authority over my life. Get out of my life now, IN JESUS NAME,for I am set free!

<u>See next section for answers to chapter questions.</u>

HELPFUL ANSWERS TO CHAPTER QUESTIONS

CHOOSE TO CHANGE YOUR DESTINY

Chapter 1

1. Present

2. Good, bad

3. Think

4. C. We could believe it as true, and find out how to put on the armor of God to protect ourselves. The more information that we have, the better equipped we are in dealing with spiritual forces.

5. Thoughts

6. Defeated

7. Accepting Jesus Christ

EMOTIONAL EFFECTS ON THE BODY

Chapter 2

1. Recall.

2. Answers from the book are: Fear can bring on heart palpitations and anxiety attacks, sad or hurtful experiences produce tears, anger can raise the blood pressure, embarrassment causes the face to flush, funny and unexpected surprises make us laugh, and joy brings on a smile.

3. Yes

4. Yes. Yes

5. Yes, yes

RECOGNIZING THE ENEMY

Chapter 3

1. Yes

2. No

3. Life, death

4. Satan, Satan

5. No. 1st Timothy 2:14 tells us she was deceived. She did not know that the serpent was an enemy or she would not have listened to him.

6. Yes

7. Word

8. Submit, resist, flee

WORDS RELEASE POWER

Chapter 4

1. Yes

2. Yes

3. God, God

4. Yes

5. Desires

6. Essay question – your own personal testimony

EXISTENCE

Chapter 5

1. The answer is B, by the attracting force (magnetic pull) between them.

2. False

3. God

4. The answer can be any story where a miraculous change took place without the help of human hands to alter chemical or atomic substances.

UNIVERSAL LAW

Chapter 6

1. Faith

2. B and D

3. Force

4. Reaction

5. True

6. Continue

PUTTING THE LAW OF FAITH INTO ACTION

Chapter 7

1. Yes

2. Hoping

3. Attract

4. True

5. It will continue to happen.

6. Yes

7. Yes

FOCUS CAN MAKE A DIFFERENCE

Chapter 8

1. Fear, worry

2. Thoughts

3. A. Take the focus off of what you don't want with another thought.

4. Opposite

5. Substance

6. Read, study, research

7. Focus

GIVE GOD THE REMOTE CONTROL

Chapter 9

1. A. Overlay, B. Safe, C. Attract, D. Evil spirits

2. They believe and tremble.

3. They pull down strong holds, cast down imaginations and bring thoughts into captivity to the obedience of Christ.

4. Yes, they both deal with attracting and repulsing forces.

5.Do

6. Yes

7. Love

8. Magnify

FOCUS ON WHAT YOU WANT THINGS TO BE

Chapter 10

1. Results

2. Yes

3. They were intimidated by the enemy. They allowed thoughts of defeat dominate their thinking.

4. The giants were more like grasshoppers because the Israelites would have had God on their side and He is bigger and more powerful than anything in the world.

5. God

6. Focus

7. True

8. Yes

TIME AND ETERNITY

Chapter 11

1. Light, light

2. Yes

3. False

4. The disciples were allowed to physically touch him. In Luke 24:39, Jesus said, "Look at my hands and my feet. It is I myself! Touch me and see, a ghost does not have flesh and bones, as you see I have."

5. Age or die (either answer is okay)

6. Yes

7. Confirming

8. Yes

GOD'S SON

Chapter 12

1. A. Jesus

2. False. It is not automatic. The scripture tells us that eternal life is only for those who believe in Jesus. Where one spends eternity is up to each individual.

3. False. Adam activated the curse.

4. No. Her chromosomes did not supply the Y chromosome for him to be born a male. It could only come from his father.

5. Yes, John 3:16 says, "For God so loved the world, that He gave his only BEGOTTEN Son...". In this scripture, begotten means unique or conceived from God.

6. A. Adams' action caused a reaction in the laws that govern our universe. Jesus produced another action that caused a reaction in the laws that govern our universe. Jesus paid the price for the crime.

7. Yes, through the Holy Spirit.

THEIR PLAN

Chapter 13

1. Unite

2. Blood

3. Deliver

4. Sin, death

5. Unite

6. Heaven, Earth

7. When sinners repent, there is joy in the presence of the angels. It is even more understandable when you continue reading the rest of the chapter in Luke.

8. Yes

9. A will and testament is in force only when somebody has died. It does not take effect while the one who made it is living.

10. Yes to both questions, according to Hebrew 9:15-18.

THE INVISIBLE REALM

<u>Chapter 14</u>

1. True

2. body

3. Yes

4. True

5. Universe

6. Jesus

7. The Spirit of God or the Holy Spirit.

BY HIS SPIRIT

<u>Chapter 15</u>

1. Born

2. Heirs

3. Power. (In the Greek it is "dunamis" which means the kind of power to reproduce itself.)

4. Language

5. Help, help

6. He helps us in living our own lives (we are not alone and he can give us guidance). He helps us with our loved ones who may be far away. He is not limited. He can be anywhere, anytime and do anything.

7. Can't

JOY IN HIS PRESENCE

<u>Chapter 16</u>

1. False

2. B. Tongue and heart

3. When we <u>speak</u> Gods Word for our own lives, we are causing or allowing him

to speak through us, with us, and for us. It is the two of us <u>speaking</u>. We are activated the original words spoken and inspired by God. We are letting the Holy Spirit use our mouth to release his power which is backed by all of Heaven and its angelic host.

4. Seek first the kingdom of God.

5. Joy

6. Satan

7. Yes

8. Look up more words similar to praise and their definition such as admire, commend, honor acclaim, approve, respect, like, appreciate.

ITS NOT TO LATE

<u>Chapter 17</u>

Bonus question - Personalize your own conclusion regarding faith substance.